# The Spread of Yield Management Practices

Fabiola Sfodera

(Editor)

# The Spread of Yield Management Practices

The Need for Systematic Approaches

With 9 Figures and 13 Tables

Physica-Verlag

A Springer Company

Dr. Fabiola Sfodera
Centro Italiano di Studi sul Turismo
e sulla Promozione Turistica
Via Cecci, 1
06088 Sta. Maria degli Angeli – Assisi (PG)
Italy
f.sfodera@cstassisi.it

ISBN-10   3-7908-1582-9 Physica-Verlag Heidelberg New York
ISBN-13   978-3-7908-1582-5 Physica-Verlag Heidelberg New York

Cataloging-in-Publication Data applied for
Library of Congress Control Number: 2005926778

Physica is a part of Springer Science+Business Media

springeronline.com

© Physica-Verlag Heidelberg 2006
Printed in Germany

Cover-Design: Erich Kirchner, Heidelberg

SPIN 11401803        43/3153-5 4 3 2 1 0 – Printed on acid-free paper

*Intangibility*

# Preface and introduction

*npoquT, goxop*

Yield management has always been considered a technique for large companies, whether these be airlines, railroad, car rental or hotel companies. Its application to the small and medium sized businesses that characterise the tourism industry in many countries, Italy in the first place, has never been totally excluded, but its implementation and subsequent actuation has always been considered too expensive for this type of business. In recent years all this has been changing. Technology and research have opened up new possibilities for its application at costs, and following methods, that are acceptable even to those who cannot access sophisticated statistics or mathematics instruments.

The evolution and the rapid changes in the reference scenarios both of the demand and the offer, have done the rest. It has become clear that to compete in a market as vast as the tourism one, one must apply the principles and techniques of marketing to produce and deliver a service that can satisfy the needs of the client better than the competition. In the same way, however, a deeper knowledge of the processes of the clientele's choice, acquisition and consumption permits the formulation of increasingly accurate forecasts of their behaviour and an understanding of the significance and importance that each client segment attaches to the purchase and consumption of a particular service. In this way the application of the yield management technique has assumed a new and more important position as well as a greater and constant spread. It has become clear that, moving from a marketing point of view. It is possible to satisfy the clients' needs better and, at the same time, appropriate a part of their revenue, by asking the highest price that each is willing to support to acquire a specific product or service. From a scientific viewpoint this makes it possible, even in the tourism sector of restaurant and hospitality businesses, to reconcile product differentiation with price discrimination.

The application of product differentiation is typical of competitive market forms in which the product is mature. Though marketing processes and actions aimed at differentiating their products, suppliers seek on the one hand to prolong the products' lives and on the other, much more important, to create and operate in differentiated forms of polypoly markets which allow suppliers to increase the manoeuvre margins of the price variable and, therefore, of revenue. The final goal of price discrimination, in addition, is the application of different tariffs for the same product or service in order to maximise the producer's revenue to the consumer's disadvantage according to the philosophy of applying the highest price to each market segment that it is willing to pay. The high intangibility condition of tourism services leaves space for numerous and diverse perceptions of the quality of the services acquired, corresponding to different levels of satisfaction and fidelity. In the same way the purchase of such services takes place, generally, in places other than where they will be consumed and the price, in the lack of the necessary information for formulating a correct and precise evaluation, still represents an important indicator of the quality level that can be expected. Today such considerations assume greater value, because of the introduction of a single currency in the European Community where it is now possible, in this way, to compare the price of each service with the quantity and quality of services offered and distributed using a single common denominator: the Euro. Expert forecasts of market trends indicate possible future mutations in the direction of tourist flows, not just by extra-community nations, but also within the Community itself. Tourism operators will find themselves faced with a much larger reference market than that present up until January 2002. In this context the quality/price ratio assumes greater importance in tourism choices than ever before. From a scientific viewpoint two areas have assumed very great importance in business discipline: that of *differentiation/specialisation* and that of *client relations management*. Product differentiation and production specialisation will lead to the creation of an offer that is increasingly centred in one or more highly compatible market segments and spread over an increasingly vast territory.

The increased competition for each segment will also tend to reduce gross operating profit, unless the producer manages to communicate (and the user perceives) the uniqueness of the offer. The yield management technique combined with communications targeted for each segment will not only allow the correct evaluation of the quality-price ratio but also self-selection on the part of the clientele according to the parameters defined and the segments determined as targets. The second trend is also closely connected to the strategic management of customer satisfaction and, therefore, to the survival of the business. It is a question of activating information tools through which it is possible to enhance the information available to the tourism business, derived from continuous and constant contact with its clients, in order to create a product "tailored" to their requirements and to the desire to satisfy their needs. Such systems in their most advanced forms become customer relationship management (CRM) tools and an excellent reference for the application of yield management.

What instead remains unexplored, and which can no longer be ignored, is the role of the yield management function in business organisation and in the organisational chart. In fact, in the face of numerous technical and operational problems yet to be studied, little has been written on the implications in terms of business organisation and work management. These brief considerations help us to place the yield management technique within the development and growth policy of a marketing oriented tourism business, thus rising to the role of a decision-making technique rather than a merely managerial or informational one.

From an academic viewpoint the main institutions and university centres of European tourism have begun in recent years to study its applications, keeping in mind the particular and varied organisational and managerial structures of European businesses as compared to American ones where yield management was initially applied (not only because it was introduced by American Airlines but also because the first tourism-hospitality businesses to apply it were American hotel chains).

The various evolutions and problems in the application of yield management are discussed each year during the International Conference on Yield and Revenue Management which in 2000 was held in Assisi at the Italian Centre for Advanced Studies in Tourism and Tourism Promotion (Centro Italiano di Studi Superiori sul Turismo e sulla Promozione Turistica - CST). CST was founded in 1982 as a high level centre for the training of future managers in the hospitality, food service and travel and tourism sector in Italy and in Europe and since 1993 it has become the headquarters for a university diploma programme (now the short degree programme) in Economics and Management of Tourism Businesses and of a Specialisation Degree Programme in Economics of Tourism under the Faculty of Economics of the University of Perugia. Since then much has changed and tourism has become an industry to which increasingly sophisticated research and development tools can be applied which go beyond the political boundaries of a State or a single business or groups of businesses. The work published here is the fruit of the interaction of the academic world, that of large software companies, which possess and create the technology used by tourism businesses, and the actors themselves of the Italian and international tourism sector. An excellent moment of comparison and evaluation of the gaps existing between theorisation, the modelling of a yield management system and its concrete application with all the objective and subjective limitations deriving from operational reality.

The book is divided into three parts, each of which constitutes a group of articles.

The first part, entitled "Some strategic aspects for a YMS implementation", analyses strategic aspects in relation to the implementation of a Yield Management System and is divided into five papers.
The first paper, entitled "Yield management in advanced systems of hotel management" by Fabiola Sfodera, considers YM with regard to the models and organisational set ups of hotel businesses. The paper analyses, first of all, the mains causes for lack of success in the application of yield management systems, and then places this in relation with organisational set ups that are widespread in tourism-hospitality businesses. In this way the characteristics of the mixed system, called "traditional", are analysed as well as the role of yield management in this system; a more advanced form of organisation is then analysed, that is, that of organisational learning and of its capacity to strengthen the role and function of yield management; finally reaching the most advanced organisational form, still rarely found in practice, which is that of the learning organisation which manages to develop yield management potential to the maximum as a management

technique and not merely a technique for the definition of prices and the optimisation of revenue. The paper ends with the formulation of four different scenarios of the evolution of yield management and of their applicability.

The second paper, entitled "How to yield value: the Janus perspective" by Brian Parry and David McCaskey, analyses the implications deriving from the application of a yield management system in budget hotels, a form of hospitality that is increasingly widespread in England and in Europe. Taking their cue from organisational and operational problems encountered in actual practice, the authors evaluate the advantages of Yield Management, both from an organisational point of view, expressed in terms of the profit margins that can be generated, and from a strategic viewpoint, in terms of image management and price communications with a view to the financial management of the business. The purpose is to quantify yield management's capacity to influence the determination and evaluation of commercial policies.

One of the main critical points for success or failure in the activation of a yield management system is staff motivation, participation and involvement. This is the topic of the third paper of this section "Human issues and the introduction of a yield management system. A case study of a 4* Chain Hotel", by Bob Brotherton and Rebecca Turner. The authors conducted a survey of the staff of the hotel chain under study after the implementation of a yield management system. This survey allowed the gathering of important qualitative data which, in part, confirm what has been examined for some time in literature and, on the other hand, reveal new important aspects connected to the motivation, participation and involvement of human resources for the success and functioning of the new system.

In recent years the analysis of the application of YMS to the restaurant sector has made advances in scientific literature, more because this sector is closely related to the hotel sector and because its offer fulfils the requirements for the application of such a system, than for any strong need expressed by the market. Nevertheless, following the first analyses and applications there is today considerable attention on the part of sector operators to the implementation of this technique in order to gather the more important advantages that it is able to offer. The fourth paper concerns strategic aspects of the application of yield management in particular with regard to the clients' perception of the variability of price in the case of brand restaurants. The paper "Yield Management and trust: the effect of variable pricing on consumer trust in a restaurant brand" by Una McMahon Beattie, Adrian Palmer, Patrick McCole and Anthony Ingold, explores a further possible limitation of relationship marketing paradigm and YM systems, namely that individual price discrimination may be perceived by buyers as undermining trust in a service provider, and thereby undermining the sustainability of a relationship.

In an analysis of the strategic implications of YM a front-line role is assumed by the control system that can be activated in the hospitality system. This is the topic of the fifth paper entitled "Controlling the yield management process in the hospitality business" by Paolo Desinano, Maria Stella Minuti and Emanuela Schiaffella. The paper is organised into a section describing the general control architecture and, after some general considerations about forecasting and room inventory control, in four subsequent sections that treat specific issues regarding the phases in which the control process can be articulated. A final section summarises the topics discussed.

The second part of the book, entitled "Yield management: new applications", groups four papers on new or innovative applications of yield management. In particular the novelties reported here are related to the application of yield management to theme parks and recreational-cultural centres and to restaurants. The first paper of this section, entitled "Revenue management in visitor attractions: a case study of the EcoTech Centre, Swaffham, Norfolk" by Julian Hoseason, analyses the case of the EcoTech Centre starting with marketing, management, functional and organisational problems to reach the implementation and application of the YM system. The in-depth study of the problems of Yield Management application in Italy is the topic of the paper entitled "Revenue management and food service businesses: the case of Italy" by Emanuela Schiaffella. "Recent events, challenges and options in revenue management" is the title of the paper by Paolo Desinano which has the aim of pointing out some emerging issues that pose new challenges to Y&RM theory and practice.

The application of YM to the restaurant sector, as evidenced in the first section of the book, is the topic of analysis, verification, testing and application. Nevertheless there are many aspects which still require analysis, testing and theorising Some of these are the subject of the paper "Revenue management in the restaurant sector" by Charlotte R. Rassing, a prelude to a practical, detailed and precise analysis.

The third section of the volume, entitled "Information instruments for a YMS in the hospitality industry", is dedicated to an analysis of the characteristics, problems and implications involved in the definition, creation and use of software necessary for the application of YM in the hospitality sector. For this reason we felt it to be useful to include the testimony of two of the main producers of YM software: Microsoft Fidelio and IDeaS Inc., Integrated Decisions and Systems.

This volume is the work of numerous persons: of the authors and of all those who contributed to the organisation and realisation of the "Fifth International Yield and Revenue Management Conference" in 2000, entitled "The spread of Yield Management practices the need for systematic approaches" which was the inspiration and starting point for this book. Special thanks to Helen Sullivan Sini, without whose patient revision many inaccuracies would not have been eliminated, and to Stefano Guarnello who handled the layout.

Particular thanks go to CST – Centro Studi sul Turismo di Assisi and to its direction, for its farsightedness and constant commitment, both economic and of human resources, in research and innovation in the tourism sector which has made the realisation and publication of this book possible.


Fabiola Sfodera
Marketing Area
Centro Studi Superiori sul Turismo – CST
Assisi – Perugia – Italy

# Table of contents

## Human issues and the introduction of a yield management system. A case study of a 4* Chain Hotel
by Bob Brotherton and Rebecca Turner

## Yield management and trust: the effect of variable pricing on consumer trust in a restaurant brand
by Una McMahon Beattie, Adrian Palmer, Patrick McCole and Anthony Ingold

## Controlling the yield management process in the hospitality business
by Paolo Desinano, Maria Stella Minuti, Emanuela Schiaffella

# Part II – Yield management: new applications

## Revenue management in visitor attractions: a case study of the EcoTech Centre, Swaffham, Norfolk
by Julian Hoseason

## Revenue management
## in the restaurant sector
by Charlotte R. Rassing

## Revenue management and food service
## businesses: the case of Italy
by Emanuela Schiaffella

## Recent events, challenges and options
## in revenue management
by Paolo Desinano

# Part III - Information instruments
# for a YMS in the hospitality industry

## Microsoft Fidelio: Opus 2 overview
by Opus 2 Revenue Technologies

# e-yield™ technical brief
by IDeaS Inc., Integrated Decisions and Systems

# Part I

# Some strategic aspects of a YMS implementation

# Yield management in advanced systems of hotel management

**Fabiola Sfodera**

f.sfodera@libero.it

CST – Università di Perugia

Via C. Cecci, 1 – 06088 – Assisi (PG) – Italy

## 1 Abstract

What is the position of yield management in hotel business organisations? What is its potential? Is this totally achieved or is there still an unexpressed margin? And with what organisational form does yield management best develop its potential? Innovations regarding organisational structure and work organisation in hotels have placed in doubt the role and position which yield management currently holds in hotels. This paper analyses, first of all, the principal causes for the failure of yield management systems and then relates these to the organisational structures widespread in the tourism-hospitality business. In this way the characteristics of a mixed or traditional system are analysed, along with the role that yield management plays in it; we shall also analyse a more advanced form of organisation, that of organisational learning, and its ability to strengthen the role and function of yield management, to the point of reaching the most advanced organisational form, still rarely recognisable in practice, which is the learning organisation which manages to develop to the maximum the potential of yield management as a management technique and not merely a technique for the determination of prices and the optimisation of revenue. The paper ends with the formulation of four different scenarios for the evolution of yield management and for their applicability.

# 2 Introduction

Increasingly one witnesses the failure of yield management applications in hotel structures. The analyses conducted in Italy through the research and degree theses prepared at the Italian Centre for Advanced Studies in Tourism of Assisi (CST) and those published in the principal sector journals[1], have demonstrated that the main causes of failure in the implementation of a yield management system are:

1.  an inadequate information system;

2.  the crystallisation of the current organisation. Often it is not adapted for the functioning of the yield management system, an added activity in the organisation;

3.  non-incisive training: just techniques. The entire organisation is not trained in the implementation of the system. Only the staff directly involved are taught the software application;

4.  the marketing objectives are unclear and segmentation not well defined;

5.  difficulty, for independent hotels, in defining the standard product upon which yield management is applied;

All these causes have something in common: they refer to the difficulty in conceiving yield management as a management technique which in order to function needs to be absorbed into the business organisation. It also modifies the commercialisation processes. In fact, as a technique, merely recognising its existence and training staff in the application of the software is not sufficient to guarantee the success of yield management. These are required and necessary activities. Nonetheless they do not guarantee that the technique becomes an instrument of successful management.

This paper does not intend to investigate any single cause for failure among those listed, this has already been done, but rather how yield management is collocated within the business organisation of a hotel. In particular we wish to analyse:

1.  the position of yield management in advanced organisational systems;

2.  the new way of planning a product in the experience economy;

---

[1]  In particular we refer to the article of Lieberman W.H, Debunking the Myths of Yield Management, which points out 10 myths to be discredited. These myths are: myth 1 YM is a computer system; myth 2 YM takes control away from employees; myth 3 YM works only when demand exceeds supply; myth 4 YM is price discounting; myth 5 YM is incompatible with good customer service; myth 6 YM is too complex; myth 7 YM doesn't address "my" problems; myth 8 YM programs automatically increase revenues; myth 9 hotels using YM don't need to change a thing; myth 10 hotels can't use YM if competitors don't. The Cornell H.R.A. Quarterly, February 1993, pages. 34-41

3. the way in which this technique must be modified or adapted to the new models for the organisation of work in businesses.

In recent years, in fact, in the hospitality sector certain important changes have occurred which represent opportunities for reaching and maintaining competitive market positions.

The importance of these opportunities varies in relationship to the degree of competition in the market in which one is operating. These can be summarised in two trends of innovation. The first is that of the techniques for the management, running and organisation of hospitality businesses. The second is related to the re-definition and re-engineering of the hospitality product in the experience economy.

These are two aspects which have an effect on the operability of hotel management, from the moment of its creation to that of daily activity, conditioning the entire organisation, the application of instruments and the techniques of management. It is exactly for this pervasive capacity in the entire structure that it also conditions the applicability of yield management.

In the world hospitality panorama the first applications of more complex managerial systems based on the principles of the learning organisation[2] can already be found but, on the whole, these are innovations which, still, cannot be found in the majority of cases.


# 3 The evolution of the organisational structure of the hospitality business

## 3.1 The mixed organisational system and the model for the planning and control of strategic management

The organisational structure currently most widespread is a mixed one deriving from the integration of the functional model with the divisional model. The purpose is that of maximising the advantages deriving from functional specialisation with those coming from a full-field vision of the divisional organisation. It is by now standard practice to speak of hotels thinking of the individual departments that compose them: rooms division, F&B, accounting, etc. a practice consolidated also by the techniques for monitoring operational costs

---

[2]   In particular we refer to the Starwood group which has introduced the Six Sigma system as the instrument of advanced managerial control based on the principles of the learning organisation. Bruno Cavasini, "L'apprendimento dinamico nel sistema Six Sigma", tesi di laurea triennale in Economia e Gestione dei Servizi Turistici, Università degli Studi di Perugia, Assisi, 2003.

deriving from the ABC system of industrial accounting. A *strategic management* system of planning and managerial control, based on the implementation of planned behaviours and their constant control aimed at gathering environmental discontinuities to obtain additional successes, corresponds to the mixed organisational structure. Strategic management has substituted strategic planning since the first half of the 1980's as a system able to foresee and incorporate the environmental variable as a strategic planning variable. The speed with which change occurs in tourism and hospitality businesses, in particular, cannot be overlooked. Flexibility has become an important objective which all firms, that wish to compete in these fields, must reach. In particular strategic management is based on decision-making processes for which:

- the solution found is satisfactory in that moment and in that condition, even if it is not considered optimum;

- the strategy is a system of acts and reports and not the single output of a formal process.

The compatibility and coherence of the two decisional axioms of the strategic management system with yield management can be seen immediately. Even for yield management the solution proposed, and that is the individual price classes and the prices applied to individual clients, is the most satisfactory solution in that moment and under those operational conditions. In other words, it is not an absolutely valid and always applicable solution, but presumes a dynamic interaction with the external environment. In the second place, the strategies identified are not the output of a formal planning process. Unlike strategic planning, which follows a rigid planning outline, in a strategic management system the strategies are defined on the basis of the actions and the relations to activate to reach the objectives. Here there is the use of *ex ante, in itinere* and *ex post* control instruments, which help to verify the coherence of the strategies defined with the objectives set in relation to the changes which have taken place in the external environment. In particular the strategy control action is developed around three aspects:

1. *feedback of the plan*: the essence of this control is to reconfirm organisationally that the critical assumptions of the strategy, with relation to the environment, are still valid. The objective is to confirm the crucial essence of the given strategy and to keep the strategy itself running. Should the hotel have a yield management system, this control verifies if the conditions for applicability of yield management to the various demand segments determined as the target market have remained unvaried or not. Noticing a variation in the behaviour of a market segment or finding a new segment can mean the non-applicability of the revenue management strategies set and the need to activate a second level control such as the one described in the following point;

2.  *guidelines for the organisation*: This type of control is intended to verify if the direction taken leads to the real achievement of the objectives or if it is necessary to adjust the trajectory of the strategy or decide, with relative certainty, on a new strategic direction. This happens through the selective *monitoring* of market requests and *of the external environment besides the internal one*, allowing the formulation of hypotheses on further developments of the *scenarios*. With reference to yield management, this type of control verifies if the strategies for maximising profits and the assumptions on which the strategies are based are still valid and can still be applied. Unlike the first type of control, which takes into consideration the actuation of strategies, in this area both the coherence of the yield management model implemented with the objectives set and the expediency of adjusting this are evaluated;

3.  *organisation check*: this type of control *selects* the set of internal variables and of the inter-relations among these which are the basis of the strategic process and which are essential to reach the objective and, therefore, for carrying out the strategy. This is generally structured as monitoring which evolves to become a system for monitoring management and the various parts of the organisation. The organisation check is the most advanced control of the strategic management system. It verifies the expediency of the yield management system in the business context but above all how it has been inserted within the organisation and what flows of relations have been activated. In other words it verifies the operational conditions of the yield management model implemented and how it and the persons involved in its actuation interact with the rest of the organisation.

In the traditional organisational model and in the planning and control system of strategic management, yield management finds two different collocations in the business organisational chart, with reference to two different methods for its application and connotation.

The first, by now practically abandoned, envisions yield management as a line function of the rooms division, directly controlled by the "hotel director", who interacts with Reception or with the booking office, if this exists. The connotation and application of yield management in this case are practically null, highly conditioned by the understanding which individual workers have of this system to the point of making it lose its identity as a technique to become an operational instrument. Application carried out using this hypothesis have proven disastrous and represented the first cases of failure of yield management, due mostly to the difficulty in understanding how the system functions and to its real integration with the business organisation and to the models for the management and running of the hotel.

The second is currently the most wide-spread and envisions yield management as an activity of the staff belonging to the marketing & sales division. In this case yield management is envisioned as a technique of sales, of management of the offer and of sales prices.

Nonetheless even this collocation presents some risks:

-   as a staff function, it is in direct support of the direction but carrying it out is an operational function which requires interaction with the rooms division;

-   the objective of yield management is the maximisation of revenue, nevertheless it is well-known that its application must take place with a view to the long range rather than short range effects. Should this not happen it could, in the long run, damage the image of the hotel without leading to an effective increase in revenue. For example, when yield management with high season prices is applied to habitual clients who are also present in the structure in low season; or when the communication to the clients is not clear and such to permit them to justify the different economic treatment received.

This need and this awareness have caused a nearly total shift of yield management toward the marketing area, causing the problems connected to the interrelation of the system with other company functions to become of secondary importance. In particular with the Reception (for the management of communications), with Housekeeping and Maintenance (for the reordering of rooms) and with the company information system (for the gathering and circulation of information). The risk, in this case, is that yield management become a system for the exclusive use of the marketing function and of the direction and, as something that rains down from above, that it have an effect on the actions and behaviours of others without their having any voice in the matter. This situation represents a risk in the case that the organisation is leaning toward the sharing of knowledge to make this a common good, intending by this not so much the sharing of data and information useful for carrying out one's work, but rather of values, procedures and know how.

In neither case does yield management succeed in fully developing its potential as it could if inserted in an organisation by processes.

In fact, yield management is a strategic activity which to function requires the activation of a two-way communications process among the departments in which it interacts. Even in the tourism business, notoriously labour intensive, but also a sector of small family-run businesses, the awareness is rapidly spreading that traditional management models can no longer develop sufficient knowledge, values, and competitiveness to compete both in the current model and in the future scenarios that are developing.

For this reason for some time it has become vitally important to study in depth the concepts, instruments and techniques of mature economic sectors.

This trend regards not only management, with the development of managerial models for conducting business rather than family ones, and marketing, which puts competitive instruments in play in mature markets such as product differentiation and brand policy, but also the organisation, which is evolving from the traditional form to models which tend toward the learning organisation, as the ultimate expression of an efficient and effective business organisation model.

## 3.2 Organisational learning: a very near reality

The passage from the mixed organisation to organisational learning in the tourism business has barely begun, yet those who have embraced it are already able to profit from its advantages. As always when changes take place, these are dictated by need and by the impossibility of carrying out one's job as one has always done, with the same satisfactory results. When this is no longer possible, change toward new models and new systems has already begun.

This is what happened, at the time, to the model for business planning based on a static and formal approach (strategic planning) in favour of strategic management, mentioned above, and it is what is happening now to strategic management in favour of *dynamic learning*. The reasons for this evolution must be sought, first of all, in the changes which have taken place in the external environment, and that is those in relation to:

- the globalisation of the market, intending by this both economic progress, the broadening of the physical market and the competition, and the virtualisation itself of business;

- the centrality of the time factor which becomes a strategic variable of business planning. The great dilemma that has characterised the last decade of the past century is exactly that related to the role of time, to its priority and compatibility with the quality of the work carried out or of the service offered. The turbulence of markets and of the phenomena which directly or indirectly affect the tourism sector require here, more than in any other economic sector, problem solving ability, that is the ability to make decisions in little time and in conditions of uncertainty. This has meant that the time variable, in many cases, becomes even more strategic than quality. In other words it is better to finish a job in time or make a decision rapidly rather than be certain of the quality of a job done or the validity of a decision but arrive late. These are also the operational conditions of yield management in which the seller must communicate the price to a client who is on the phone, quickly deciding which tariff to apply, keeping in mind the information to hand about the occupation trend on the same day of the previous year, of the price classes available and of the segment to which a client hypothetically belongs and whom the seller only knows from a brief telephone conversation. With yield management, the situation is even more complex because one must respond in little time and, at the same time, communicate a tariff that is adequate to the characteristics of the client, with the risk, should that not happen, of losing him/her. Thus the importance of having information and adequate instruments available but, especially, of having a structure behind one which can place the strategic decision-making dimension in relation with the organisational one in a dynamic logic.

In relation to these changed conditions of external operability the limits of strategic management have become insupportable. And this must be sought in:

a. *insufficient ability to adapt* of the model which cannot grasp opportunities for change different from those which are part of the adaptation logic of the model itself;

b. *insufficient control system* as an instrument of adaptation since it is still only an instrument of comparison between what has been delivered and what was planned, and because the external analysis is carried out on selected factors offering the possibility of interpreting the present and predetermining the planned future without representing an intuitive guide for what does not yet exist and has not been foreseen.

The connection between the strategic dimension and the organisational one allows this limit to be overcome and to approach a system of management, planning and control that is dynamic and competitive, in which workers feel themselves to be an integral part of the whole, and of which they share values and principles. This connection is realised, as mentioned above, in *dynamic learning*.

To obtain this, first off, the meaning itself of work in a hotel must be modified. No longer a series of tasks defined in a job description in which each division defines its activity and puts to use its experience but making knowledge explicit which becomes a dynamic growth element.

Above all it belongs to all, in the logic of group learning which lies at the base of organisational learning.

A hotel organised in this way will be a hotel in which the staff does not participate in training courses for individual divisions or because required by the direction but it will be a hotel in which the initiative and experience of persons can be put to use, for example through the development of internal projects, and hopefully become the knowledge and shared "patrimony" of the entire structure. In such a hotel the turnover will be low because people will feel motivated since they can combine their own personal growth to that of the structure in which they work which will also give them interesting professional opportunity for satisfaction, growth or specialisation.

Always in such a hotel, yield management is not a term that the majority do not know about nor a technique that is the sole prerogative of marketing or booking but rather a process in which knowledge and information flow from the various divisions and whose actuation improves the satisfaction of the hotel and its employees and increases knowledge and the ability to satisfy the clients.

### 3.2.1 Conditions for the application of organisational learning

To understand the passage from a traditional organisation (whether this be mixed, divisional or purely functional) one must first analyse the elements that are essential for organisational planning, that is:

a. *the coordination mechanisms* emphasise the importance of the organisation also as an instrument of communications and control besides for the division of work, as was pointed out previously. Coordination mechanisms, according to Mintzberg, include: direct supervision, the standardisation of work processes with the predetermination of behaviours, the standardisation of input, including the specification of the abilities and knowledge required, and reciprocal adaptation;

b. *The parts making up an organisation*, which include the general management, the operational area, the intermediate line of connection, the techno-structure for interventions of standardisation and the support staff which carries out activities not directly connected to the operational flow.

The various organisational set ups depend on the configuration of the coordination mechanisms and on the different roles carried out by the individual parts of the organisation, all in relation to the external and internal operational situations. In organisational learning the coordination among the various elements of the organisation is high and of a relational nature, as is communication which uses both formal and informal channels, and control takes on the characteristics of operation and strategic control.

The component parts of the organisation communicate at different levels using adaptation and the coordination mechanism, enhancing at the same time innovation and specialisation. This organisational model has been adopted by some important hotel chains which make coordination, communications and strategic control the instruments for an innovative and dynamic management of their hotels.

We can summarise the most important concepts of organisational learning by pointing out the difference between individual learning, typical of traditional organisations and organisational learning:

1. *individual learning* enriches the knowledge and skills of an individual who can make these available to a community.

2. *learning within an organisation*, which is no longer individual but of the organisation itself, creates the basis and the substratum upon which all the knowledge and the various possibilities for choice of the organisation as a whole are based.

Organisational learning is a process through which the organisation itself acquires, transforms and matures new knowledge, new abilities, new skills based on collective experience. Learning that can develop is called organisational and is greater than the sum of individual learning. The know how, skills and knowledge have value because they are shared, assimilated and redefined within the organisation. Knowledge is a good of the organisation that remains with it even when an individual leaves the firm, since part remains within.

### 3.2.2 Yield management in organisational learning

In a more evolved organisational context even yield management develops great potential for success both because it has a more adequate system available for the organisation of work which is able to create the optimum conditions of applicability, coherently with the external environment, and because it can interact, in the logic of processes, with the other functions, transferring concepts, practices and information which can improve individual performance.

The organisation context for the application of yield management in this case requires that the parts of the organisation start up a synergic process for the acquisition of *information and knowledge*, and then *interpret* and *distribute* these, in a coordinated manner within the structure in order to *retain* and *memorise* whatever can determine an increase in competency. In other words this means that in this context Reception, Booking, Accounts but also Breakfast, the Bar and all the other services available in the hotel will acquire the information and knowledge necessary to give life to a yield management system, besides Marketing which will be concerned both with internal information and with the external market information. This information and knowledge will then be interpreted and distributed within the hotel: to Reception, for example, so that they can communicate correctly with the clients; to Booking so that they can determine with a brief conversation the characteristics of the potential client; or whether the person is a habitual client, and therefore define the class to which s/he belongs and the price to propose; to Accounts so that they can process bills, combining client identification codes or the segments to which they belong in order to know the average expenditure of each type of clientele; Food & Beverage, Breakfast, the Bar and all the other services can have useful information on the behaviour of the clientele, on their needs and their purchase and consumption methods to, in turn, apply yield management.

This useful information is maintained and memorised within the structure and equipment of the divisions or offices which can draw benefit from it in more efficiently carrying out its own activity. Yield management becomes an instrument for the growth of the organisation, in which the persons and the activities directly or indirectly involved are informed and contribute to giving life to the process necessary for its functioning. It is no longer a software, a sales technique or another invention of Marketing and of Management to maximise profits but it now becomes a management technique.

# 4 The learning organisation: an objective to be reached

Organisational learning represents a very up-to-date business organisational model in the hotel sector toward which both the large international chains and individual independent hotels, which occupy positions that are by no means marginal in the market, lean. The advantages of organisational learning are undeniable, even for yield management application purposes, as has been shown above. Nevertheless, when an organisation makes all the learning processes a strategic lever of value and, therefore, a central element of its planning and of its continuous re-planning, it passes from a common condition, which is that of organisational learning to that of the *learning organisation*.

The organisation itself becomes capable of learning, places under discussion the values that regulate it and the objectives set and not just the strategies. That is, it places itself in a dynamic condition before the market and its internal structure is characterised by people who, in carrying out their work, do not ask themselves simply *how to do something* but also *why*. What characterises this organisational context is the investigative curiosity which demonstrates itself under the form of the continuous search for relations, explanations, cause and effect and which draws its origin from delegation, decentralisation and empowerment. The focal element of an organisation that is able to learn is the conviction that from interaction and exchange among the various parts of the whole, synergies can be generated and more information and more articulated knowledge can be produced which in turn foster a proactive culture. Eliminating, or in any event reducing, resistance to change and the search for innovation generate a lever effect able to sustain and amplify the development of the knowledge and skills possessed and to facilitate, thanks to the control processes which distinguish each incremental process, the continuous and progressive improvement of the organisational structure attained at the moment.

The application conditions of the learning organisation and its characteristics can be summarised as follows:

- it encourages creativity and initiative. The learning process itself is the object of a learning process. The possibility of improving one's own work and the ways in which it is conducted is an important lever of manoeuvre with employees who qualify their jobs on the basis of the personal satisfaction, not just economic, that they draw from it. For this reason empowerment, delegation and decentralisation are fundamental conditions for the existence and success of an organisation able to learn. They must be placed in the field at the right moment and managed as a motivational lever able to reduce the high turnover that characterises hotels.

- it is concerned with the climate and quality of the work environment. As already mentioned, the work environment of a hotel organised according to this model is positive, the climate is relaxed, there is cooperation, enthusiasm, a desire to grow and improve. Employees are ready to become the protagonists of their own work and not just persons carrying out orders and this especially for the more strictly operative activities. A valuable connection is established between the learning process and the innovation process. Those who enter a learning organisation find themselves in an environment intent on growth, on experimentation and innovation in which it is only natural to reduce or lower one's defences against change and in which each person's contribution to the organisation and to the collective learning becomes part of the organisation itself and stays there even after that person has decided to change jobs. It is the most important solution to the problem of loss of skill and know how deriving from the high turnover which afflicts hotels and which is also one of the principal causes for the lack of success of yield management system applications.

• it sustains and supports the development of teamwork activities and of the values of collaboration which foster social interaction and the birth of new ideas. The groups become excellent instruments to support the dynamic dimension of learning.

• It sustains and increments the implementation of Information and Communication Technology (ICT) to guarantee a continuous and constant flow of information.

These conditions and characteristics are also the conditions for the success of a yield management system.

## 4.1   Yield management in the learning organisation

The application of yield management in the learning organisation is still an open question, as much from a theoretical-conceptual point of view as from the operational one. What appears evident is that in the learning organisation there has been an ulterior evolution of yield management, of its applicability and application and, especially, of its role within the organisation.

In a learning organisation the application of yield management can challenge not only the way of acting, modifying sales techniques, the relations and coordination among the various divisions involved, but it can also challenge the behaviours in act and their underlying values. In other words it can challenge the philosophy, the business culture and the very concept of one's job.

From crossed analyses of the characteristics of the learning organisation with those of yield management it has been possible to trace some scenarios for the future of yield management application in a learning organisation, and that is:

1. the most extreme scenario is one which leads to the non applicability of yield management when this is in conflict with the philosophy, the concept of

hospitality and the very essence of the hotel. In a learning organisation each action, behaviour and activity is realised coherently with the essence of the hotel itself which defines its principles, business culture and values. Should price discrimination be in conflict with the essence of the hospitality and welcoming of the hotel, yield management becomes inapplicable. The organisational learning behaviours generated would push work organisation in a direction that is incoherent with the philosophy of the hotel.

2.  a second scenario is that of the evolution of yield management to the point of making it an instrument for the personalisation of prices in an organisation able to create and provide clients with unique experiences. In the economy of experiences the purchase choice and consumption methods are defined by what one wishes to experience. What hotels are proposing to their clients are no longer rooms and some accessory services but living experiences, unique and worth talking about, made up of the coherence and integration of the entire offer. In this scenario price discrimination, at the root of yield management, is no longer applied to standard rooms but to the experiences offered to the market and which include, besides the room, all the additional services able to create and make the experience live. Certainly its application becomes more complicated but it will present greater advantages from the point of view of communications and client satisfaction. To apply yield management in a context such as this, the organisation must have a high degree of coordination and must be able to learn and modify, if necessary, even the principles and the organisational set up itself, besides the values.

3.  the third scenario places a stronger accent on the marketing component, modifying the order of priority of segmentation variables. The variables that allow the hotel to recognise the behaviour of the individual segments faced with price discrimination based on the economic concepts of marginal utility become more important. The target market will in this way be composed of market segments expediently combined according to this end.

4.  in the last scenario hypothesised, yield management loses its strategic connotation to become a simple technique to apply in support of the reception or booking staff. No correlation, no process, no staff function, no provisional system but simply an instrument in support of the definition of prices to apply which remains the object of the individual and collective learning of the organisation itself. This does not mean that there are no yield management applications, but that each hotel can design the model of yield management that is most suitable and appropriate for its needs and objectives.

# References

Argyris C., Schon D.A., (Italian versione edited by Xarmagnola F. and Tomassini M.), *Apprendimento organizzativo*, Edizioni Angelo Guerrini e Associati SpA, Milano 1998

Belobaba P.B., *Back to the future? Directions for revenue management*, Journal of Revenue and Pricing Management, Vol. 1 No. 1, 2002, pp. 87-89

Cavasini B., *"L'apprendimento dinamico nel sistema Six Sigma"*, tesi di laurea triennale in Economia e Gestione dei Servizi Turistici, Università degli Studi di Perugia, Assisi, 2003)

De Simone Niquesa L., *Economia e direzione delle imprese ricettive e ristorative*, Franco Angeli, Milano, 2003

Frank S., *Applying Six Sigma to revenue and pricing management*, Journal of Revenue and Pricing Management, Vol. 2 No. 3, 2003, pp. 245-254

Kuhlmann R., *Future of revenue management – Why is revenue management not working?*, Journal of Revenue and Pricing Management, Vol. 2 No. 4, 2004, pp 378-387

Lederer P. and Yeoman I., *The natural extension of marketing*, in Journal of Revenue and Pricing Management, Vol. 2 No. 1, 2003, pp. 81-82

Lieberman W.H., *Debunking the myths of Yield Management*, The Cornell H.R.A. Quarterly, February 1993, pp. 34-41

Minzberg H., *La progettazione dell'organizzazione aziendale*, Il Mulino, Bologna 1985

Noone B.M., Kimes S. E. and Renaghan L. M., *Integrating customer relationship management and revenue management: a hotel perspective*, Journal of Revenue and Pricing Management, Vol. 2 No. 1, 2003, pp. 7-21

Peroni G., *Marketing turistico*, Franco Angeli, Milano, 1998, VII ed.

Pinchuk S., *Revenue management's ability to control marketing, pricing and product development*, Journal of Revenue and Pricing Management, Vol. 1 No. 1, 2002, pp. 76-86

Pinchuk S., *Revenue management's ability to control marketing, pricing and product development: Part II*, Journal of Revenue and Pricing Management, Vol. 1 No. 1, 2002, pp. 174-182

Pinchuk S., *Revenue management does far more than manage revenues*, Journal of Revenue and Pricing Management, Vol. 1 No. 3, 2002, pp. 283-285

Pande P.S., Neuman R.P., Cavanagh r.r, *The Six Sigma Way*, McGraw-Hill, New York, 2000.

Sfodera F. *Dispense del Corso di Economia e controllo manageriale delle imprese ricettive e ristorative*, a.a. 2003-2004, Università degli Studi di Perugia, Facoltà di Economia, Corso di Laurea in Economia del Turismo

Shoemaker S., *Future of Revenue Management – The future of pricing services*, Journal of Revenue and Pricing Management, Vol. 2 No.3, 2003, pp.271-279

Wirtz J. Kimes S. E., Ho Peng Theng J. and Patterson P., *Revenue management: Resolving potential customer conflicts*, Journal of Revenue and Pricing Management, Vol. 2 No. 3, 2003, pp. 216-226

# How to yield value: the Janus perspective

**Bryn Parry**

Southampton Business School
Southampton Institute
East Park Terrace
Southampton, SO14 0RH
United Kingdom


**David McCaskey**

Centre for Management Studies
Colchester Institute
Essex, CO15 6JQ
United Kingdom

*Contents: 1 Introduction. 2 Operational Y.M. issues. 2.1 The rapid expansion of budget hotels. 2.2 The effect of economic cyclicality on the decline. 2.3 Non-price variables gain importance in selection criteria. 3 Strategic Y.M. issues. 3.1 Mission. 3.2 Funding philosophy. 3.3 Creating value – in the eyes of the market. 4 Concluding debate. References*

# 1   Introduction

A prescient comment from the floor at the *4ᵗʰ Annual International Yield and Revenue Management Conference* posed the question what does one do when everyone is utilising *Yield Management [YM]*? This paper takes up that challenge and integrates the operational implications of *YM* into the strategic perspectives of hospitality organisations. Recognising that one needs to seek out a suitable framework for analysis (Bettis & Prahalad)(Phillips, 1998), this paper takes a systems approach (Johns & Jones, 1999a&b) (Forrester, 1995), addressing through-lifecycle issues (Langston, 1999) (Parry, 1999a). Recognising that any 'Hospitality system' is governed by feedback loops (Senge, 1990) – this paper addresses a simple acid test for the effectiveness of *YM,* namely its ability to influence and determine commercial valuations (Marshall & Williamson, 1994) (Heer & Koller, 2000) (Hsu & O'Halloran, 1997).

Put another way, this papers seeks to address the most effective blend of:

1. **Operational *YM* issues:** *e.g.* the sustainable profit levels that a company can generate;

2. **Strategic *YM* issues**: *e.g.* the image perceptions driving the `*exit multiple*' of those profits; which underpins the company's financial engineering.

Given the comments above, the definition of *YM* adopted by this paper will be:

"A management technique by which an organisation's decision-making process actively utilises information affecting the factors driving the demand patterns for, and supply costs of, the central product [e.g. accommodation] - in order to optimise the return from total sales (in the short, medium and long term)" (Parry, 1999b).

Figure 1: Janus perspective

# Yielding Value

Operational                                 Strategic

*Yield Management*               *Yield Management*

Issues                                    Issues

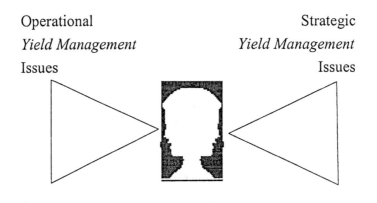

Market Environment

# 2  Operational Y.M. issues

Looking forward into the new millennium there follows three '*emergent*' issues which had limited influence in the 1990s, but which will have a significant impact in the next decade - on *Yield Management practise*, in the UK and on European hotels.

1. The rapid expansion of Budget Hotels.

2. That the effects of economic cyclicality - a major industry driver and yield factor - are on the decline.

3. That research continues to show that non-price variables are gaining in importance, at the expense of price, in selection criteria.

## 2.1  The rapid expansion of budget hotels

*HVS International* (2000) recorded the following from a *Dow Jones* news report. The UK's growing budget sector could erode the market share and profits enjoyed by the mid-market operators such as *Thistle, Regal* and *Jarvis. Merrill Lynch* expects the number of budget hotel rooms to rise from 40,000 in 1999 to 80,000 by 2003, accounting for 20% of the UK hotel market. *Whitbread* announced that it would be developing a network of *Travel Inns,* alongside *Punch Taverns,* in an £80 million joint venture. Similar expansion schemes are expected from the other major operators, such as *Granada, Bass, Accor* and *Premier*.

The voracious "*Pac Man Effect*" of this rapid growth of budget hotels, initially estimated by McCaskey (2000), has been recalculated using *the Merrill Lynch* forecast:
40,000 rooms [at an average inn occupancy of 80%] = 32,000 room nights
Multiply by 366 nights (leap year) = 11,712,000 annual nights
In 1995, *Kleinwort Benson* estimated that = 30.25 million room nights
*UK Plc* hotels sold in 1996, 31.35 million room nights

So, in excess of 35 per cent of demand is currently being gobbled up by these newcomers and - given the estimated doubling in supply by 2003 and accounting for some growth in demand - budget hotels could, by then, have captured over 55 per cent of UK room nights. Whilst some of this demand may have been cannibalised from the existing brands of the major *Plc* operators, much of it is being taken from the smaller groups and unaffiliated hotels who in the past drew from this market segment.

Traditional 2/3 star hotels are vulnerable, as they have built-in cost structures that are high. The new lodge formats, meanwhile, have a low-cost base - a parallel may be drawn with low-cost airlines, which have recently gained significant market share to the detriment of existing carriers. Comparison shows that low-cost airlines achieve a similar demand mix to lodges – 60 per cent *Leisure* to 40 per cent *Business*. Mason (1999) found a number of contemporary studies that suggested that pressure is being brought to bear on business travellers to reduce travel expenditure; he cites *IATA* (1997), Bender and Stephenson (1998) and Mason (1998).

A similarly explosive growth in lodge provision in the USA, between the mid-1960s and the late 1970s, left many of their unfocused mid-market hotels in disarray. In the air, deregulation spawned the growth of low-cost airlines which helped to rapidly bring about the demise of *Pan Am* and *TWA*. This process is now in full spate in the UK and Europe and is having a radical dampening effect on prices and subsequent yields in both industries (*Airbus Industrie*, 2000).

## 2.2 The effect of economic cyclicality is on the decline

Research published in *"Leisure in the New Millennium"* report (*Henley Centre, 2000*), for the *Joint Industry Hospitality Congress [JHIC]* conference, showed that the link between the boom and bust cycles of the UK economy are diminishing. Hospitality, which is often seen as suffering disproportionately - being first into a recession and last out of it- appears to have finally broken away from this destructive cycle.

*Henley Centre* (2000) reported that:

- There is great potential for the leisure industry. It is already one of the largest sectors of the economy, and is one of the very few large sectors to have strong growth. Growth will come from an increase in discretionary income, in particular from the wealthy grey market.

- What people do with their free time is becoming more important to their identity than what they do for a living. There are early indications that this will mean that leisure expenditure will become more resilient during any future down turns in the economy.

- Consumer expenditure seems to have become less prone to the boom-bust cycles. Modelling consumer expenditure over the last ten years shows a strong correlation between leisure expenditure and key economic indicators such as prices unemployment etc. ... however these models have started to lose their predictive capability: where once the industry was heavily dependent on the economy, now it seems to be developing some independence".

Leisure expenditure used to be thought of as a luxury; increasingly it is becoming an essential. Henley identified this as 'sanity expenditure'.

In his conference speech, Philip Monks (2000) [of *Barclays Bank Plc*, sponsors of the *Henley Report*] assured his audience that *Barclays* was now committed to being a major player in the hospitality industry. It had commissioned this report to help it understand how the industry works and this had much altered the banks' perception of the industry in particular of its associated risks.

The main finding was:

"...that economic downturns affect the industry no more severely than business in general. They may even have less severe effects at times. So we need to have a less negative reaction to such downturns."

Slattery (1996), in describing the future as "*a golden age for hotels*", predicted this uncoupling of the economy from hotel demand. He also projected the de-seasonalisation of demand patterns with through-year demand being generated, by the expanding grey market – which, increasingly, had the time, money and inclination for hotel stays. This segment would also eliminate the predictable weekend troughs and dead Sunday nights, as they indulged in three-day weekends.

It would seem that some of those demand factors which have invoked much *YM* application are becoming less prevalent and, whilst it's not entirely good bye to weekend troughs, seasonal highs and lows, all tied to the helter-skelter of the UK economy, their impact is diminishing rapidly.

## 2.3 Non-price variables gain importance in selection criteria

In his examination of aspects of "*Pricing a Service*", Ken Irons (1993) found that in most markets, indeed in the majority of markets as far as the Western world is concerned, non-price variables are gaining at the expense of price.

"That this had been happening for some considerable time and has been forecast as a outcome of economic progress for at least the past 60 years. As people become more used to economic power, the focus will move from basic to higher needs, a direct echo of Maslow's theory of the hierarchy of needs. In such circumstances, the importance of relating both price and quality to consumer needs, as they see it both from their expectations and experiences, is clearly critical and the extremely low emphasis on price is evident from our core respondents."

Much has been written about branding as a major, non-price, variable and influencer of choice criteria.

To illustrate this, the marketing practises of the *Whitbread Hotel Company*'s *Travel Inn* brand will be integrated into the "*Seven Characteristics of Leadership Brands*" [adapted from Tilley (2000)]. *Travel Inn* is the outstanding market leader in the burgeoning lodge sector; achieving 86 per cent room occupancy, across its 220 outlets, in 1999 and an astounding 78 per cent repeat occupancy (McCaskey, 1999a).

1. Rather than follow rules and markets, they create them. This is easily

illustrated by the "*Guaranteed Good Night*" scheme currently being piloted in four, representative, *Travel Inn*s: Euston, Coventry, Derby and *Nottingham Central*. Under this scheme, if you did not have a good night, you simply claim a refund. This is entirely in keeping with *Tesco*'s, mould breaking, '*Non-Smiling Fish*' guarantee - of money back, or a replacement for any product sold by them (McCaskey, 1999b). Within *Travel Inn*, "mystery shopper" grades clearly showed that this promise was operationally feasible and could be sustained; however, piloting was essential to iron out operational issues and develop implementation training. The "first mover" status that this will gain *Travel Inn* is considerable and, in the time that it takes for any fast-followers to adopt, will prove an unbeatable differentiator. Some of you may be familiar with a similar scheme, initiated by Christopher Hart [for *Hampton Inns, USA*], in 1990. Indeed, prior to its launch, Chris Hart presented details of his scheme to senior management of the *Whitbread Hotel Company* and its internal franchisees. A full account of the benefits may be found in Bateson (1995) and in Teare *et al* (1994). Today, most US lodges have introduced some sort of guarantee but, often, in a rather desultory and meaningless manner, similar to those who followed *McDonald*'s lead and put up notices that '*toilets were inspected every hour on the hour*' but which, in many cases, are obviously an empty promise.

2. They effectively create a meaning that is more than just a function of the product or service. Research showed that Travel Inn is 'more approachable than Holiday Inn Express and TraveLodge'. It, also, confirmed Travel Inn to be the 'first choice in affordable accommodation'.

3. Leadership brands embody meaning in all that they do. The whole issue of ethics and *YM* and the pluralist approach adopted by *Whitbread* is discussed in Stanley and McCaskey (1999)

4. They are consistent and eloquent in every aspect of their communication ensuring understanding. The recent, innovative, *TV* campaign fully meets these criteria

5. They are dynamic, constantly changing to meet new needs and remain relevant. The, 1998, brand re-launch, clearly redefining the brand proposition may be found in speech by [*Marketing Director*] Guy Parsons (1999) speech to the "*Marketing Week Marketing Hotels '99*" conference, where he also showed that there was a continuous dialogue between the brand and its users.

6. Leadership brands have social responsibilities; they hold beliefs, attitudes and behaviours which earn the respect of those outside. This was clearly exemplified in the speech of David Thomas (2000) [*Chief Executive, Whitbread Plc*]: " A few years back, we were criticised by some people in the hotel business, and a fair number of city analysts, for missing the opportunity

to make short term profits in Travel Inn. As you may know, we had a sin
national price and applied it every night of the week – not a pricing polic,
typical of the hotel industry. The outcome is that Travel Inn has grown to be
the UK's largest branded hotel network with almost 250 hotels and 12,500
rooms, Occupancy is running at 86% across the brand – a record for the UK
and our returns continue to rise – it's a win win for our customers and
ourselves."

7. Their leadership is earned not given. Leadership brands permeate the whole
   organisation, they are not just its label. They provide a living template of how
   to act, what to do for the best and how to move into the future. For *Whitbread*,
   David Thomas concluded: "My message is a simple one. Our customers are
   well informed and have plenty of choice. They shop around for good value. If
   we provide it they'll reward us – and in turn this enables us to reward our
   shareholders who include most of our staff". *Whitbread* is well spoken of by
   hotel users in general and is well respected in the industry.

The intention here is not to infer that price does not matter but that it is often not
the deciding influence; in many cases the confident expectation of a well-
established brand will override.

To show that price matters, one only has to witness the furore of activity under the
banner of *'Rip Off Britain'* which has successfully targeted, retail banking, super-
marketing and motorcar distribution, as having unfair pricing policies.

It has to be stated that there are aspects of pricing in our industry - such as:
inflated rack-rates; *bait and switch* advertising; single room supplements; kick-
backs to agents / intermediaries and to their staffs; etc. - which are entirely
questionable and, given the current consumer rights-driven agenda, will,
inevitably, be exposed in the media.

To avoid censure, test the validity of your pricing against the following criteria:

- It should be Mainstream, Competitive, Universal, Consistent, Fair and Easily
  Communicated (Stanley & McCaskey, 1999).

# 3 Strategic Y.M. issues

In March 2000, *Olympus Real Estate*, of Dallas, Texas, U.S.A., spent $1 million
on buying the *Rockresort* brand name; even though: "*The brand owned no
properties, held no management contracts it was just a name*" (Jeffer et al., 2000).

Justifying the purchase, Eric Prevette argued that:

"With more consumers attracted to this niche, we're confident that we will capture
more than our fair share of the upper end leisure market. There may be

consolidations down the road, but for now we feel at ease with the current dynamics and how our skill set will enable us to succeed" (Jeffer *et al.*, 2000).

The price paid for the "*goodwill*" of this company demonstrates that more is required of effective *YM* than just effective forecasting and operational skills. Companies will need to blend their strategic *Mission* (Katzenbach & Smith, 1994) with their funding philosophy (Clayton *et al.*, 1999) (Wagle, 1998) and their ability to create value, in the eyes of the market (Economist, 2000).

## 3.1 Mission

In order to ensure that operational *YM* advantages are translated, effectively, into bottom-line profits, it is vital that the company's *Mission, Objectives, Strategy* and *Tactics* are streamlined.

The *Ashridge mission model* (Stacey, 1993) helps to highlight areas of tension and potential improvement. *YM* must not fall prey to over-simplified *Missions* (Bartlett & Ghoshal, 1994) or mixed-messages (Bucklin *et al.*, 1997) within the organisation [and its supply chain (Heape, 1994)]

Figure 2: Ashridge mission model

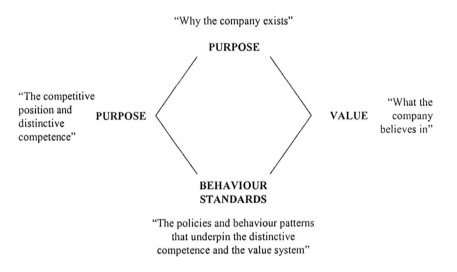

## 3.2 Funding philosophy

Recent attempts to develop innovative methods of funding – such as *Real Estate Investment Trusts* [*REITS*] (*King Sturge*, 1998) (HIO, 1998), or the securitisation of investments (Wilder, 1998) (ICCL, 2000), favoured by *Nomura* – have not proved to be the radical developments promised. They do, though, serve notice that an organisation that adopts a radically different funding philosophy will operate different *YM* parameters. Swig (1999) suggests redefining the mature hotel sector and its funding is an obviously overlooked aspect. Parry (1999a) indicated how market perceptions can put a sector out of favour with key investors, something which many commentators felt happened to the UK hotel sector during the late 1970s and early 1980s. Companies willing to accept higher risks, investing over longer time periods, or achieving lower investment / operating costs, will be able to out-manoeuvre the average hospitality company. Quek & Henry (1998) illustrate that capitalisation rates for *US* hotels have been consistently higher than other real estate investments, because of concern over the cyclicality of the profit / income stream. They go on to observe that:

" ...in a recent survey of investor perceptions, PKF Consulting found that full-service luxury hotels and upscale hotels were perceived as the most favored property types, while economy limited-service hotels ranked as the least popular with investors".

Hence, whilst improving operational *YM* issues might help the fulfilment of investments, more effective strategic *YM* would enable the identification and education of the key stakeholders who can influence the investment structure's long-term benefit for the hospitality company.

PKF (1999) found that "historically, management tends to underestimate its forecasts of occupancy growth, while overestimating its ability to raise room rates and profits". Whilst, resonating with other research on risk-taking, removing the inherent errors caused by such a culture would reduce a company's operational challenges, as well as improving its relative attractiveness to investors.

## 3.3 Creating value – in the eyes of the market

Jarvis (1995) warned that using *YM* techniques to out-source under-performing areas of a business would lead to its demise; a view taken up by Ghoshal *et al.* (1999). The *Economist* (2000) demonstrates the relevance of this, to the topic at hand. *Bass* sought to leave the, under-valued, UK brewing sector and refocus the group, as befits the world's second largest hotel group (Hotels, 2000).

Despite this: "....Bass's shares still track Britain's depressed brewing sector. In the past five years the shares have underperformed Marriott, Granada and Accor by 30-45% and the overall British stockmarket by 40%." (Economist, 2000).

Although operational *YM*-based techniques have helped to improve profits from *Inter-Continental* hotels, by 60 per cent, *Gross Operating Margins* are still some six percentage points below those achieved by *Hilton* hotels. A low share price would make *Bass* more reliant on loans and investors might be concerned that half of those profits come from just four, booming, cities [London, Paris, New York and Chicago] (Economist, 2000). Hence, by not balancing operational *YM* activity with strategic *YM* components [*e.g.* investor loyalty, risk philosophy, brand equity and share values], *Bass* seems to be working hard to hold back its full potential.

# 4 Concluding debate

In his critique of three articles (Johns & James, 1999a&b) (Johns & James, 2000), on the application of systems to the hospitality, Kirk (2000) argues that when we talk:

"Catering systems or in this instance of Yield Management Systems or Property Management Systems the approach has been one of simplifying problems in a reductionist way. Treating all problems as if they were ones of cause and effect thus describing the outcomes we may have a system but it is not generated using a general or soft systems methodology".

The new methodology calls for this deductive methodology to be subsumed by an inductive approach. This allows a break away from models of causality and should result in the use of systems concepts as a means of understanding complex issues. This paper is an attempt to codify the components that will enable a complex, holistic, framework to be developed – drawing on systems theory (Forrester, 1995) outlined in earlier work (Parry & Norman, 1996).

Whilst focusing on *YM*, this acknowledges work by others – *e.g.* Philips (1998), Kaplan & Norton (1993) and *Arthur Andersen* (2000).

The simplistic valuation matrix in *Appendix A* can be used to illustrate key issues raised and to focus delegates' debate: operational *YM* decisions should be profit-focused and, so, strengthen the profit-stream during the important first five years. If the *YM* techniques are focused only on the short-term, though, these profit levels will not be sustained throughout the asset's life;

- operational *YM* decisions must reflect their impact on strategic issues [*e.g.* brand equity; value for money; *etc.*], or the organisation / unit will struggle to sustain the top-end *exit multiples* - which underpin strong market values, high share prices, advantageous credit ratings, *etc.*;

- strategic *YM* decisions should help to achieve advantageous interest rates and risk components;

- effective blending of operational and strategic *YM* components should ensure that the organisation makes the most of market opportunities and optimises the value achieved.

It is for these reasons that future research will tend to apply soft systems methodology to *Yield Management* issues. Checkland and Scholes (1999) indicate

that:

"The concept itself starts with the basic thinking that a system may have properties which refer to the whole and are meaningless in terms of the parts which make up the whole. These are the so-called emergent properties, i.e. the sum is more (or less) than the sum of the parts."

The concept of emergence implies a view of reality as existing as layers in a hierarchy; to which are added the concepts of *Survival, Communication* and *Control* – thus, creating a *complex adaptive system* (Beinhocker, 1997).

# References

Airbus Industrie, *Global Market Forecast*, 2000, 31707 Blagnac Cedex, Airbus Industrie. Available at: http://www.airbus.com.

Arthur Andersen, *Value Creation Framework*, 2000. Available at: http://170.253.125.61/valuedynamics/image_bkgd0510v6.html

Bartlett C.A. & Ghoshal, S., *Beyond Strategy to Purpose*, Harvard Business Review, Nov. – Dec., 1994, pp. 79 – 88.

Bateson J., *Managing Services Marketing*, 2nd Ed., London, Dryden Press, 1995.

Beinhocker E., *Strategy at the edge of chaos*, McKinsey Quarterly, Number 1, 1997, pp.24-39. Available: http://mckinseyquarterly.com.

Bender A. & Stephenson F., *Contemporary issues affecting the demand for business air travel in the United States*, Journal of Air Transport Management V$^{ol.}$ 4 N$^o.$ 2, 1998, pp. 99-109.

Bettis R.A. & Prahalad, C.K., *The Dominant logic: retrospective and & extension*, Strategic Management Journal, John Wiley and Sons, 1995.

Bucklin C.B. *et al*, *Channel conflict: when is it dangerous ?*, McKinsey Quarterly, Number 3, 1997, pp. 36 – 43. Available: http://mckinseyquarterly.com.

Checkland P. & Scholes J., *Soft Systems Methodology in Action*, Chichester, Wiley, 1999, pp.18-19.

Clayton J., Gambill B., & Harned D., *The curse of too much capital: building new businesses in large corporations*, McKinsey, quarterly, Number 3, 1999, pp.48 - 59. Available: http://mckinseyquarterly.com.

Economist, *Room for Reservations*, Economist, London, 1st July, 2000.

Forrester J., *The beginnings of Systems dynamics*, McKinsey Quarterly, Number 4, 1995, pp. 4 – 16. Available: http://mckinseyquarterly.com.

Ghoshal S., Bartlett C.A. & Moran P., *A New Manifesto for Management*, Sloan, Management Review, Spring, 1999, pp. 9 – 20.

Heape R., *Outward Bound*, Tourism Society Journal, Vol.83, 1994, pp.4-5., in Law, E., "Perspectives on Pricing Decision in the Inclusive Holiday Industry", in Yeoman, I. and Ingold, A. (Eds. 1997), "Yield Management: Strategies for the Service Industries", London, Cassell, pp.67-82.

Heer M.D. & Koller, *Valuing cyclical companies*, McKinsey, T.M. quarterly, number 2, 2000. Available: http://mckinseyquarterly.com.

Henley Centre For Forecasting, *Leisure in the New Millennium Report*, Cranfield, 2000, Barclays Bank / JHIC / Henley Centre for forecasting.

HIO, *Three Years and $5 Billion*, Hotels Investment Outlook, 18th June, 1998, pp.18-26.

Hsu W. & O'Halloran, *The Hong Kong Hilton: the case of the disappearing hotel*, Cornell Hotel and Restaurant Quarterly, August, 1997, pp. 46-55.

Hotels, *Hotels' 325* survey, Hotels, July, 2000. Available at: http://www.hotelsmag.com/PDF/0700hotgiants.pdf

*HVS, Hospitality E News*, 14 July 2000. Available: enews-europe@hvsinternational.com.

IATA, *Cost conscious business travellers will try non frill airlines*, IATA Press Release No. PS/13/9, International Air Transport Association, 27th January 1997, in Mason K.J., 1999, "The Propensity of Business Travellers to use Low-cost Airlines" discussion paper, Cranfield, Cranfield University.

ICCL, *Securitisation – a growing trend*, International Centre for Commercial Law, 2000 Available at: www.icclaw.com/devs/uk/ma/ukma_030.htm

Irons K., *Managing service companies*, London, Addison Welsey, 1993, pp. 198-199.

Jarvis P., *Contracting Out Facilities and Services Affects Fixed Asset Valuation*, Public Eye, 14, Oct - Dec, 1995, pp. 2 - 3.

Jeffer, Mangels, Butler & Marmaro, *Olympus Making Bold Moves*, Hotel Online special report, 2000.
Available at: www.hotel-online.com/Neo/News/PressReleases2000_1st/Mar00_JMBM Prevette.html

Johns N. & Jones P., *Systems: mind over matter*, Hospitality Review, July, V[ol.]1 N[o.]3, 1999.

Johns N. & Jones P., *"Systems and management: the principles of performance"*, Hospitality Review, October, V[ol.]1 N[o.]4, 1999.

Johns N. & Jones P., *Systems and management: Understanding the real world*, Hospitality Review, January, V[ol]2 N[o] 1, 2000.

Kaplan R.S. & Norton D.P, *Putting the Balanced Scorecard to Work*, Harvard Business Review, Sept-Oct, 1993, pp.134 – 142.

Katzenbach J.R. & Smith D.K., *Teams at the Top*, McKinsey Quarterly, N° 1, 1994, pp.71-79. Available: http://mckinseyquarterly.com.

King Sturge, *REITs coming your way soon ?*, London, King Sturge, July, 1998.

Kirk D., *The value of systems in hospitality management*, The Hospitality Review, April, V[ol]2 N[o] 2, 2000.

Langston J., Keynote speech, *Eighth Annual CHME Hospitality Research Conference*, Guildford, University of Surrey, 1999.

Marshall H. & Williamson H., *Law and Valuation of Leisure Property*, London, Estates Gazette, 1994.

Mason K.J., *Corporate involvement in short haul business travel markets in Europe*, unpublished PhD thesis, Faculty of Science, University of Plymouth, in Mason K.J. 1999, "The Propensity of Business Travellers to use Low-cost Airlines" discussion paper, Cranfield, Cranfield University, 1998.

Mason K.J., *The Propensity of Business Travellers to use Low-cost Airlines*, discussion paper, Cranfield, Cranfield University, 1999.

McCaskey D., *Yield Management and Ethics; An Oxymoron* ?, Hospitality, July/August, 1999.

McCaskey D., *Customer, Customer, Customer,* Hospitality, October, 1999.

McCaskey D., *The future is polarised*, Hospitality Review April, V$^{ol.}$2 N$^{o}$ 2, 2000.

Monks P., *Speech to the The Customer Has Arrived, Let's Face It* conference, Joint Hospitality Industry Congress [JHIC], Gloucester Millennium Hotel, London, 7$^{th}$ July, 2000.

Parry, *Understanding the Language of Recession – interpreting business cycles*, in Lockwood, A. (Ed.) proceedings of "Eighth Annual CHME Hospitality Research Conference", Guildford, University of Surrey, 1999.

Parry, *Clustering in Las Vegas*, in McCaskey, D. (Ed.) "4$^{th}$ Annual International Yield and Revenue Management Conference proceedings", Colchester Institute, Clacton, 1999.

Parry B. & Norman P., *Facility Performance in the European Hospitality Industry*, "*EuroFM / IFMA 1996 Conference*" proceedings, Barcelona, May, 1996, pp.417 – 432.

Parsons G., *Expanding the Market* in "Marketing Week Marketing Hotels '99" conference, Café Royal, London, June, 1999.

Philips P., *Strategic Planning Systems in Hospitality and tourism*, London, CABI, 1998.

PKF Consulting, *Preserve Occupancy at All Costs* ?, Pannell Kerr Forster Consulting, Atlanta, March, 1999. Available:
www.hotel-online.com/Neo/Trends/ PKF/Special/ManagersShare Plans_May99.html.

Quek P & Henry L.E., (Cap) *Rating Perceptions of Risk*, Pannell Kerr Forster Consulting, Atlanta, June 1998.
Available: www.hotel-online.com/Neo/Trends/PKF/Special/ CapRating_ June98.html.

Senge P., *The Fifth Discipline: the art & practice of the learning organisation*, London, Century Books, 1990.

Slattery P., *United Kingdom Hospitality Review*, Kleinwort Benson Research, London. 1996.

Stacey R.D., *Strategic Management and Organisational Dynamics*, London, Pitman, 1993, p. 329.

Stanley P. & McCaskey D. *Yield and revenue management in budget hotels* in McCaskey, D. (Ed.), *Proceedings of The Fourth Annual International Yield and Revenue Management Conference*, Colchester Institute, Clacton, 1999.

Swig R., *Redefining a mature hotel sector*, International Society of Hospitality Consultants, Memphis, December 1999.
Available: www.ishc.com/library/redefining.html

Teare R. et al, *Marketing in Hospitality and Tourism*, London Cassell, 1994.

Thomas D., *Speech to the The Customer Has Arrived, Let's Face It* conference, Joint Hospitality Industry Congress [JHIC], Gloucester Millennium Hotel, London, 7<sup>th</sup> July 2000.

Tilley C., *Built-in Branding,* Journal of Marketing Management V$^{ol.}$15 N$^{os.}$1-3, Jan-April, 1999, pp.181-191.

Wagle D., *The case for ERP*, McKinsey Quarterly, Number 2, 1998, pp. 131 - 138. Available: http://mckinseyquarterly.com.

Wilder, J., *Hotel Securitisation,* 1998. Available: http://www.innvest.com/news/library /articles/finance/HotelSecuritizaion.htm

# Human issues and the introduction of a yield management system. A case study of a 4* Chain Hotel

**Bob Brotherton and Rebecca Turner**

Department of Hospitality and Tourism Management
Hollings Faculty
The Manchester Metropolitan University
Old Hall Lane
Manchester, M14 6HR
United Kingdom

*Contents: 1 Introduction. 2 Methodology. 3 Literature review. 4 The case study. 5 Conclusions and recommendations. References*

# 1  Introduction

Many commentators on Yield Management (YM), for example, Rowe, (1989); Brotherton and Mooney, (1992); Harris, (1995); Yeoman and Watson, (1997); Donaghy et al, (1997); Lee-Ross and Johns, (1997), have stressed the importance of considering the 'people element' in hotels seeking to adopt a YM system and its associated business philosophy. In spite of this hotel companies invariably either ignore, or relegate to a subsidiary consideration, the fundamental human issues such a change inevitably generates.

The introduction of a Computerised Yield Management System (CYMS) involves far more than those logistical and technical changes to existing systems required as an integral element of this process. Such a change not only alters the nature of the capacity management infrastructure within the hotel, it also impacts on the work roles, mindsets and behaviour of reservations staff, their relationships with customers, and how they perceive the operation of a YM-driven environment.

It is these issues this paper focuses on. The research work underpinning the paper is based on a case study approach focusing on the people issues associated with the introduction/implementation of a CYMS system in the case study hotel. A series of semi-structured interviews were conducted with some of the key personnel, at senior/line management and employee levels, involved in this process. The results obtained from this yielded some rich qualitative data indicating that there are a number of strategic and operational issues associated with the effective, or otherwise, introduction and implementation of such a change. Many of these are referred to widely in the associated YM literature but do not as yet appear to be reflected in management practice. The paper concludes by proposing a series of practical recommendations for practitioners.

## 2 Methodology

Given the existence of a reasonably substantial body of literature on yield management, a deductive approach to designing this research was considered to be the most appropriate. The initial work consisted of a review of the pertinent literature to establish the current state of knowledge on the issues that the research was to address. The results obtained from this literature review were, then, used as a basis to compile the interview questions that comprised the main empirical data collection instrument. The empirical research design constituted what Yin (1994) refers to as a 'Type 2' case study. The Type 2 design focuses attention on a single context or case, but uses multiple (in Yin's terminology 'embedded') units of analysis within this context. In this study the single case was the hotel in question with the multiple units of analysis, comprising the levels of employees interviewed.

This design was considered appropriate for this research as it enabled the researchers to explore the issues in some depth within the case situation.

The sample chosen for the interviews included representatives drawn from senior management, line management and front-line employees as follows:

Senior Management

- Deputy GM/Marketing Manager;
- Rooms Division Manager;
- Reservations Manager.

Line Management

- Head Receptionist;
- Reception Manager.

Front-Line Employees

- Reservations Co-ordinator;
- Receptionists.

These individuals were selected to provide a range of views from different management and employee levels in the organisation. This, in turn, enabling the researchers to explore how each level were involved in the Yield Management Implementation (YMI) process, whether there was a shared understanding of YM philosophy and the extent to which perceptions of the YMI process were congruent or otherwise. Rooms Division managers/staff were specifically chosen as respondents as the YM system currently operates only within this division. All the respondents were long-term employees and therefore regarded as ideal interview candidates due to their experience and wealth of knowledge. Once the draft interview questions had been determined, a pilot study was conducted with two of the potential respondents at the hotel to test the extent to which the questions were unambiguous and understandable. This process indicated that the terminology used in some of the questions was a little difficult to understand and these questions were re-worded accordingly. The revised interview questions were then forwarded to each respondent prior to the interview and the interviews took place in late 1999. The interview questions were mainly of an open-ended nature to encourage the provision of in-depth answers. Each interview was tape recorded to prevent distraction from note taking, encourage eye contact and the evaluation of body language. The interview questions were derived from the literature review and sub-divided into five sections to facilitate analysis and provide respondents with an indication of the key areas the study was focusing on, namely:

– Section A - Yield Management Implementation;

– Section B - Education;

– Section C - Training;

– Section D - Organisational Culture;

– Section E - Organisational Change.

The taped interviews were transcribed into Microsoft Word '97. Once transcribed, the interview responses were compared to identify the emergence of patterns.

# 3 Literature review

It is widely recognised that American Airlines successfully developed YM in the late 1970's (Kimes, 1989; Fitzsimmons and Fitzsimmons, 1998). Through the 1980's and 1990's YM has also been applied to other types of service companies such as car rental, freight transport and hotels (Kimes, 1997), cruises (Hoseason, 1999) and holidays (Edgar, 1997). The application of YM also exits on golf courses, amusement parks, tourist attractions and theatres etc., but is not extensively exploited (Anderson, 1995; Fitzsimmons and Fitzsimmons, 1998). However, the development of CYMS within hotels has been a slow process

(Rowe, 1989; Bradley and Ingold, 1993; Donaghy et al, 1997). Although technological developments have increased YM applications into hotels (Jauncey et al, 1995) the expense of investing in technology often means that CYMS mainly prevail within large hotel corporations. However, according to Anderson (1995), small and medium-sized enterprises do adopt "manual" approaches to YM, which are equally successful. To date a considerable amount of literature has been published on YM in the hotel industry. The early (1980's) articles tend to be of a descriptive/explanatory nature and were largely concerned with defining the YM concept and identifying the operational motives for its implementation. A number of empirical studies have been conducted on YM adoption in hotels. These have ranged from individual hotel case studies (Peters and Reilly, 1997; Huyton and Peters, 1997; and Jauncey et al, 1999) to research embracing several hotel contexts at once (Bradley and Ingold, 1993; Jarvis et al, 1998).

More recently specific YM issues have been researched. For example Luciani, (1999), Lee-Ross and Johns (1997), Edgar (1998) and Noone and Andrews (1999) have all examined the application of YM to small and medium sized companies. The literature has also tended to increasingly focus on the significance of the 'people element' during YM implementation processes (Jones and Hamilton, 1992; Donaghy et al, 1995; Yeoman and Watson, 1997; Hansen and Eringa, 1998; Farrell and Whelan-Ryan, 1999).

Many writers primarily regard YM as a technique to enhance profit, yield, revenue or return (Orkin, 1988; Dun and Brooks, 1990; Brotherton and Mooney, 1992; Bradley and Ingold, 1993; MacVicar and Rodger, 1996; Fitzsimmons and Fitzsimmons, 1998). CYMS are also considered alternatives to traditional forecasting techniques, where accurate forecasting is maintained by manipulating historical, current and future data (Brotherton and Mooney, 1992; Lieberman, 1993; MacVicar and Rodger, 1996; Lee-Ross and Johns, 1997). However, others suggest that such 'automated' decision-making processes should not be entirely relied on and final decisions must remain a human responsibility (Hott et al, 1989; Gamble, 1991; Jones and Hamilton, 1992; Donaghy et al 1995; Yeoman and Watson, 1997; Davidson and de Marco, 1999).

To enhance awareness of YM within hotels, skills must be developed to practice such techniques proficiently. All staff (management and employees) must be involved in training sessions, especially those dealing with sales and inquiries, to develop an understanding of its effects on their job roles and the establishment (Donaghy et al, 1995; Donaghy and McMahon-Beattie, 1998; Farrell and Whelan-Ryan, 1998; Hansen and Eringa, 1998). According to Davidson and de Marco (1999), communication and commitment must be established prior to training and education programmes commencing.

Farrell and Whelan-Ryan (1998) suggest that successful education and training programmes will be acquired by those who employ external consultants to implement the YMS. Subsequently, training should be an on-going process for all personnel, using both internal (in-house, organisation-specific) and external (YM consultants) training processes (Farrell and Whelan-Ryan, 1998). Successful YMI depends on a highly trained and motivated team, confirming that full attention must be geared towards the people element (Donaghy and McMahon-Beattie, 1998; Okumus and Hemmington, 1998). This increased emphasis on the 'human element' during YMI is featured strongly in more recent literature that, in turn, directly relates to the development of a 'yield culture'. Jones and Hamilton (1992:95) conclude that management lack effort in developing a yield culture, but also state that:

"Because YM is complex and because it depends significantly in information technology, involving people is difficult".

According to Jones and Hamilton (1992), the first stage in implementing a YM culture is ensuring everybody within the organisation understands the phenomenon. Brotherton and Mooney (1992) support this view, implying that hoteliers must concentrate primarily on people and that organisational and software programmes are less important. The planning stage in developing such cultural changes is also heavily emphasised within the literature. Organisations should develop dynamic and responsive organisational cultures with support from head office and unit managers, to enhance employee morale and motivation (Brotherton and Mooney, 1992; Donaghy et al, 1995; Farrell and Whelan-Ryan, 1998).

Internal restructuring may also need to take place when adopting cultural changes (Brotherton and Mooney, 1992; Donaghy et al, 1997; Farrell and Whelan-Ryan, 1998; Davidson and de Marco, 1999). This may involve moving offices; organising open plan offices; reformation of policies and procedures and structural changes to the organisation chart, to create flatter, leaner organisations. Successful YMI requires organisational change, communication, co-ordination and co-operation from all levels, whether at an individual, organisational or corporate level, which needs to be carefully planned and appropriately resourced (Kimes, 1989; Jauncey et al, 1995; Donaghy et al, 1997).

However, MacVicar and Rodger (1996) and Davidson and de Marco, (1999), claim staff and guests are rarely consulted during YMI's. Initiatives often fail due to a lack of commitment, which is essential for the development and control of CYMS (Kimes, 1989; Farrell and Whelan-Ryan 1998; Hansen and Eringa, 1998). Some writers claim that CYMS de-skill employees because the decision-making process is removed (Kimes, 1989; Brotherton and Mooney, 1992; Bradley and Ingold, 1993; Hansen and Eringa, 1998). Others hold opposing views, stating that technology increases skills within organisations (MacVicar and Rodger, 1996). However, a clear relation does exist within the literature, outlining the significance of fundamental, but sometimes small changes that organisations must consider during YMI. From the 'people' perspective these include:

- developing a yield culture;
- establishing a forecasting committee/YM team, including rooms, reservations, sales, marketing, food and beverage, banqueting and front office managers to meet weekly;
- developing employee commitment;
- identifying human resource implications;
- implementing incentive schemes to enhance motivation;
- providing appropriate training and education;
- clarifying interdepartmental relationships;
- amending job descriptions.

Although some writers have evaluated and established idealistic approaches for YMI in hotels (Farrell and Whelan –Ryan, 1998; Hansen and Eringa, 1998), and while theories differ, the importance of the 'people element' when implementing any organisational change is fundamentally stressed by many commentators (Rowe, 1989; Brotherton and Mooney, 1992; Harris, 1995; Yeoman and Watson, 1997; Donaghy et al, 1997; Lee-Ross and Johns, 1997; Okumus and Hemmington, 1998). Despite this, the literature generally agrees that the human element is not addressed satisfactorily within many YMI processes (Kimes, 1994; Donaghy et al, 1995; Jauncey et al, 1995; MacVicar and Rodger, 1996; McCaskey, 1998).

# 4 The case study

The case study hotel has a central Manchester location and was opened in 1992. Its facilities included 132 bedrooms, a fitness centre, two bars, conference facilities and two restaurants; a Fine Dining restaurant and French Brasserie. From the beginning, the hotel was extremely popular and occupancy levels were high.

To maintain its prestigious identity an emphasis on high standards and investment in people was established, including recruitment, career opportunities, training and development, and gradually a profile of regular guests was established. Business and corporate clients often fill the hotel midweek. As with many business-orientated hotels, demand decreases at weekends, and the leisure market is therefore targeted using special offers (lower rates) and promotions. Since opening, the hotel has undergone many changes.

In 1996 bedroom capacity was increased to 156 rooms, to coincide with the Euro '96 soccer tournament, although manpower levels have decreased from 270 to 220 employees. In 1997/8 the company owning the hotel acquired a major UK hotel company and decided to re-brand the hotel to fit into the portfolio of 4* hotels operated by this company. Following this the hotel has become increasingly profit oriented, with more emphasis on cutting costs and meeting budgets. The use of technology has also increased with the introduction of an enhanced key interface system, a close circuit television security system, pay TV and play station handsets within the bedrooms being some recent developments. More recently implementation of the Optims Yield Management System has taken place.

In September 1998 it was announced that an agreement had been signed with TIMS to implement the Optims Yield Management System into the company's 4* hotel brand world-wide (TIMS, 1998b). The hotel's system was installed in January 1999 in two phases, each with a duration of one week. Phase one, included training, site preparations and the input of history, budgets, room and yield classes into the system (see Table 1).

Table 1: Optims Phase One Installation Agenda. Source: TIMS (1998a)

| DAY/TIME | MODULE | PERSONNEL TO ATTEND |
|---|---|---|
| Monday<br>0900-1230<br><br>1300-1700 | Site Preparation, Installation of programmes & interface.<br>Review of implementation. | Systems Manager<br><br>Revenue Manager |
| Tuesday<br>0900-1230<br><br>1300-1700 | Construction of room classes<br><br>Construction of yield classes | General & Revenue Manager.<br>As above. |
| Wednesday<br>0900-12.30<br>1300-1700 | Input of room and yield classes.<br>Validate system parameters | Optims personnel<br>Optims personnel |
| Thursday<br>0900-12.30<br>1300-1700 | History/Budget Input<br>Optims Training | Revenue Manager<br>General & Revenue Manager, Director of sales. |
| Friday<br>0900-1230<br><br>pm | Front office/sales training – 2 x 1 hours sessions<br>Review and sign off | All front office and sales staff<br>General Manager<br>Revenue Manager |

Six months later, TIMS returned from France to conduct phase two of the YMI. During this time the system collected data, and TIMS supplied support and assistance through the Optims helpdesk. Phase two included training, the verification of data, forecasts, rate controls, deal quotations and demand analysis (see Table 2).

Table 2: Optims Phase Two Installation Agenda. Source: TIMS (1998a)

| DAY/TIME | MODULE | PERSONNEL |
|---|---|---|
| Monday 0900-1230 | Data verification Forecast calibration | Optims personnel |
| 1300-1700 | Forecast calibration | Optims personnel |
| Tuesday 0900-1230 | Forecast verification | Revenue & Reservations Manager. |
| 1300-1700 | Forecast training. Rate controls and capacities | Revenue Manager, Reservations Manager & Sales Manager. |
| Wednesday 0900-1230 | Forecast verification, demand analysis | Revenue & Reservations Manager. |
| 1300-1700 | Deal quotations. | Revenue Manager, Sales Manager, Conference Manager. |
| Thursday 0900-1230 | Forecast verification, demand analysis | Revenue & Reservations Manager. |
| 1300-1700 | As above | As above |
| Friday 0900-1230 | Using Optims reports. | Revenue & Reservations Manager |
| pm | Review and Sign off. | General Manager Revenue Manager. |

Within both installation agendas only senior managers were involved, and supervisors or employees are only mentioned once in the Phase One training sessions.

Although the YMI was in-depth, and could therefore justify the exclusion of a wide range of personnel, there was very little communication, tuition or training regarding the YM system during this time, or once the system was installed. There was no indication within Optim's installation agendas of strategic issues regarding the 'people element' to indicate how employees and customers should be informed of the change. However, in a report on the installation process TIMS explicitly state that staff feedback meetings should be held 'to communicate operational details of strategic planning and success of previous actions' and that 'incentive schemes should be offered regularly to operational, front office and sales staff' (TIMS, 1998a).

This leads to a consideration of the interview data. The tables that follow contain the interview responses coded according to the following key:

1. Deputy General Manager:     DGM.

2. Reservations Manager:       Res.M.

3. Rooms Division Manager:     RDM.

4. Head Receptionist:          HR.

5. Reception Manager:          RM.

6. Reservations Co-ordinator:  RC.

7. Receptionist:               R.

Although the respondents generally felt that the initial YMI process was very good (see Table 3) one of the key issues associated with a YM operation is clarity of roles and responsibilities.

Table 3: What are your feelings about the YM installation process received from TIMS?

| | |
|------|-----------------------------------------------------------------------------------------------------------------------------------------------|
| DGM. | Yes, installation was fine; the training was very detailed and very hard for everyone in the hotel. It was very long and I actually didn't attend all the sessions. |
| Res.M | **The training was excellent, yes.** |
| RDM. | Yes, it was excellent. |
| HR. | **Yes, I thought they were very good, they brought a lot of people over from France. It wasn't rushed. The support they gave was very good.** |
| RM. | *I didn't have much involvement I couldn't say.* |

In this respect, it was worrying to find that the interview respondents did not appear to have a unanimous view on the person with overall responsibility for managing the YM system in the hotel (Table 4).

Table 4: Who is the yield manager in the hotel?

| DGM. | The Rooms Division Manager. |
|---|---|
| Res.M. | We don't have one as such, although the Rooms Division Manager assumes that role with my assistance. |
| RDM. | **The Reservations Manager and I do a bit of work between us, and the Reception Manager is beginning to get involved now as well.** |
| HR. | The Rooms Division Manager, well she maintains the system. |
| RM. | **We haven't got one but the Rooms Division Manager, reservations manager and myself are involved in it.** |
| RC. | I assume it's the Rooms Division Manager and the Reservations Manager. The Rooms Division Manager is actually managing it and the Reservations Manager helps with it. |
| R. | **The Reservations Manager.** |

Perhaps this was a function of the degree of involvement the respondents had in the YMI process (see Table 5). Clarity of responsibility is also invariably associated with communication issues.

Table 5: What involvement did you have in the YM system implementation process?

| DGM. | I was trained on it and I try to pass the information I gained onto the sales office. |
|---|---|
| Res.M. | *I've had quite a bit of involvement, not as much as should take place in my role but that was due to lack of staff in my department.* |
| RDM. | A lot. |
| HR. | None at all. |
| RM. | None. |
| RC. | None, I'm just told about things as they are implemented. |
| R. | None. |

As Table 6 shows there would appear to be some dissonance between the higher levels of respondent and those lower down in the hierarchy, with the Head Receptionist and Reception Manager indicating something very different to their superiors! Not only would there appear to be some difference of opinion between the higher level managers and others on this issue of communication.

Table 6: How is YM communicated through management?

| DGM. | Through training sessions. |
|------|---------------------------|
| Res.M. | By training in front office areas. |
| RDM. | We discuss it at the Management meeting every week. We give out forecasts from the yield system in the form of a graph, so that it's nice and user friendly and easy to use. |
| HR. | I don't think it's communicated at all through management. |
| RM. | It's not. |

Table 7 also indicates the management team have not established a systematic formal meeting mechanism to discuss YM issues.

Table 7: How often do departmental heads meet to discuss YM?

| DGM. | No departmental managers, but certainly myself, the General Manager and the Rooms Division Manager talk about it daily. |
|------|---------------------------|
| Res.M. | **We don't.** |
| RDM. | I have to admit that we are not meeting as we should, we are supposed to have daily meetings. So the General Manager, Reservations Manager, Reception Manager, Rooms Manager are to meet daily to decide the plan of action for the next two days. Each day we are to discuss what the rate will be for that evening, and then every week we are supposed to discuss the following week. We have a Sales meeting where we discuss yield and the forecast once a week. |
| HR. | Not very often, just once a month. |
| RM. | *Never.* |

The literature suggests that for a YMI to be successful the organisation should take appropriate steps to manage the change process that this inevitably generates and to establish a 'yield culture' amongst employees.

This requires that the managers and staff directly involved with the operation of the YM system, and others who will be indirectly affected by it, are made fully aware of what it means to be operating in a yield-driven environment.

There is some evidence to suggest that this did take place (see Table 8) but it was largely restricted to senior management and those managers and employees directly involved in the operation of the YM system.

However, the responses in Table 9 indicate that this process has not been as successful as the management might have hoped.

Table 8: How were staff made aware of the new YM policies and procedures?

| DGM. | We have daily meetings in the hotel. We have a weekly management meeting which all Hod's and UBM's go to, and they should feed that back to their department through staff daily briefs, job chats, through memo's and staff notice boards. |
|---|---|
| Res.M. | *Through the departmental heads, team briefs and management meetings.* |
| RDM. | *Generally by forms or memo's and they are told at team briefing meetings.* |
| HR. | **The Rooms Division Manager made sure that people understood new procedures, and how important it was that what you put in is what gets passed to the YM system, so I think that has been done well.** |
| RM. | *Memo's, reception meetings, training. They probably weren't told there was to be a change. I learnt more about it, and as things change I try and tell my staff, and try and explain as much as I know, but what I don't know I can't pass on.* |

Table 9: What commitment have employees made to YM procedures?

| DGM. | The ones that are involved in it are pretty committed to it because they understand what YM is all about, but the ones that don't aren't committed because they don't understand it. |
|---|---|
| Res M. | *Management have certainly made a great commitment. Employees are getting it incorporated more into their day-to-day routine rather than showing commitment.* |
| RDM. | *Some front-office staff seem interested.* |
| HR. | There's commitment from people like the Rooms Division Manager and the Reservations Manager who are on it all the time. I think if people were made more aware of it they would want to learn more about it. |
| RM. | *I am committed to it, but none of my staff are.* |

One would also have expected the awareness building exercise to be followed up by extensive training, particularly amongst those managers and staff who are directly responsible for the day-to-day operation of the new YMS. Unfortunately this does not seem to have happened. Tables 10 and 11 show a considerable difference between the views of the Deputy General Manager and the other respondents. They also highlight the limited range of staff who have been involved in the YM training process.

Table 10: Which staff have been involved in YM training sessions?

| DGM. | Most of the staff in the hotel have. |
|---|---|
| Res M. | **Just Front Office staff.** |
| RDM. | Not many, staff generally have had initial training on what YM does. |
| HR. | All of the reservations staff have been on it, The Reception Manager has, I have, and the Reception staff have. |
| RM. | *Just me, none of my staff have.* |
| RC. | Only the initial training, briefly explaining what the system is for. I haven't been trained to use the system. When it first came into the hotel we were trained on what it's going to do, and how you use it. But I've had no training on how to use the system specifically. |
| R. | **Nothing except for that bit I had at the beginning. I've hardly had any training, and I'd be scared to touch the system in case it crashes.** |

Table 11: How have the employees been trained to use the YM system?

| DGM. | All staff went to the training, the Rooms Division Manager, the Head Receptionist, the Reception Manger and the Reservations Manager are fully trained on it and can train people on it. So new members of staff that start have a basic understanding of it, but to be fair they don't need to use it at the moment. |
|---|---|
| Res M. | Through TIMS, the Rooms Division Manager and myself. |
| RDM. | They haven't, they're not using it yet, there's only three people, myself, the Reservations Manager and the Reception Manager that are using it. |
| HR. | They haven't. |
| RM. | *Mine haven't, the Reservations Supervisor has.* |

Given the above it is perhaps not surprising that most of the respondents, with the exception of the DGM and Res.M., feel that the training provided has not developed a widespread understanding of the YM concept amongst the staff (see Table 12). In addition to the awareness, communication and training issues referred to above the literature also suggests that the embedding, and ultimate success, of a YM system can be facilitated by the provision of appropriate incentives to staff. Incentives can help to inculcate a more positive response to the new YM environment, though incentives alone are unlikely to be a sufficient motivator for staff to fully engage with this change in orientation.

Table 12: Has the training developed an understanding of the YM concept amongst staff?

| | |
|---|---|
| DGM. | No, we have 220 staff here. If you mentioned it to 200 people they would probably ask what YM is. I would hope that most of the UBM's would understand what YM is. |
| Res M. | **There is more understanding, definitely.** |
| RDM. | I think they understand it more, I wouldn't say they'd be able to answer lots of questions on it. They are probably not fully comfortable with it but there is more understanding of it. |
| HR. | I think they are quite unaware, they may be aware on a subconscious level, as they are aware of things that are happening, but they probably don't relate it to YM. |
| RM. | *No.* |
| RC. | I understand what the system says from looking at the screen, but I couldn't use it. |
| R. | **Not as much as I should really, it's still a mystery; I'm not really sure what it's all about.** |

The evidence on this aspect is a little contradictory (see Table 13) but tends to suggest that, at the very least, any positive effects derived from the incentives provided by the hotel are likely to be minimal.

Though the management appear to have a view that incentives are offered, and that these are associated with encouraging staff to use YM practices – at least indirectly if not directly – the staff have a different perception (see Table 13).

To summarise it is clear that the interview data reveals the YMI process in this hotel has not focused strongly on the human aspects of the process. It has tended to concentrate on the integration of the technical and business aspects of the YM system and relegate the human/system interface to a secondary consideration. This may have some longer term consequences.

Table 13: What incentives have been offered to encourage staff to use YM practices?

| DGM. | There's a bonus scheme running in reception where if staff sell a certain amount of rooms at a certain rate, then a bonus is paid. We change incentives all the time. |
|---|---|
| Res M. | **We have had incentives for reception staff to sell rooms in the evening at the correct rates.** |
| RDM. | We change the incentives monthly, and this month it's been restaurant bookings to yield the restaurants. In previous months it's been room sales after 6.00pm, staff got a percentage of what the room rate was, so there has been some. |
| HR. | There haven't been any incentives offered. |
| RM. | Nothing. |
| RC. | There's been no incentive ever since I've worked here. |
| R. | None. |

# 5   Conclusions and recommendations

In conclusion it has been demonstrated that the literature associated with YMI, particularly that focusing on the 'people' or 'human' aspects of this process, clearly identifies a number of what may be regarded as 'critical' issues influencing the success, or otherwise, of any given YMI. These being:

- Awareness Building and the Development of a Yield Culture;

- Encouraging Involvement and Creating Commitment;

- Initial and Ongoing YM Training;

- Effective Communication, Co-ordination and Clarification of Responsibilities;

- Organisational and Job Re-structuring;

- Motivation and Incentivisation.

Though the relative importance of these may vary from context to context and the specifics of the YM system being introduced they are, individually and collectively, likely to be strong influences on both the efficacy of the YMI process and the efficiency and effectiveness of the YM system over time. In essence they are all inextricably linked with the *planning* of such a change from its conception to final operation. The empirical evidence derived from the case study demonstrates that a number, if not all, of these issues could have been planned for and managed more effectively. In turn, this lends further support to the contentions of many commentators that the primary focus of attention in most YMI processes tends to be that of ensuring that the technical aspects of the YM system are successfully installed and integrated with the hotel's business history and objectives. Conversely, the inculcation of a YM philosophy amongst the staff who are expected to operate the system receives far less attention.

While it would be patently foolish to suggest that organisations should reduce the amount of attention, time and resources they devote to the former, greater attention paid to the latter may be expected to yield additional benefits. This partial, very rationalistic, approach to planning the introduction, installation and implementation of a YM system may result in a reasonably satisfactory outcome vis-à-vis the benefits derived from the system, as it has in the case study hotel. On the other hand, the question remains: how much more successful, in both the implementation and operational phases, would this have been if the planning conducted for it had contained a greater emphasis on the organisational and human/system interface issues such a change inevitably embodied? The practical recommendations arising from this research are therefore clear. Firstly, 'plan, plan and plan' before the initiation of the YMI appears to be a suitable mantra.

Secondly, ensure that the plan/s address the organisational and human issues associated with the change.

Thirdly, educate and train the staff in order to develop a culture that is receptive, and willing, to embrace the new philosophy and practices before they are installed. Fourthly, initiate the required structural changes and re-negotiate work role/responsibilities prior to implementation. Fifthly, provide suitable incentives to further motivate staff and secure their commitment when the system is up and running. Finally, set up effective communication structures and procedures that actively encourage staff to engage with, and contribute to, the operation of the YM system.

# References

Anderson A, *Yield Management in Small and Medium-sized Enterprises in the Tourist Industry*, European Commission Report Directorate General XXIII – Tourism Unit, 1995.

Brotherton B. & Mooney S., *Yield Management – Progress and Prospects*, International Journal of Hospitality Management, Vol.11, No.1, 1992, pp. 23-32.

Bradley A & Ingold A., *An Investigation of Yield Management in Birmingham Hotels,* International Journal of Contemporary Hospitality Management, Vol.5, No.2, 1993, pp. 13-16.

Davidson M.C.G. & De Marco L., *Corporate Change: Education as a Catalyst,* International Journal of Contemporary Hospitality Management, Vol.11, No.1, 1999, pp. 16-23.

Donaghy, K., McMahon, U. & McDowell, D., *Yield Management: An Overvie,* International Journal of Hospitality Management, Vol.14, No.2, 1995, pp. 139-150.

Donaghy K., McMahon-Beattie U. & McDowell, D., *Implementing Yield Management: Lessons form the Hotel Sector,* International Journal of Contemporary Hospitality Management, Vol.9, No.2, 1997, pp. 50-54.

Donaghy K. & McMahon-Beattie U., *The Impact of Yield Management on the Role of the Hotel General Manager,* Progress in Tourism and Hospitality Research, No.4, 1998, pp. 217-228.

Dunn K. D. & Brooks D. E., *Profit Analysis: Beyond Yield Management,* The Cornell Hotel and Restaurant Administration Quarterly, November, 1990, pp. 80-90.

Edgar D. A., *Capacity Management in the Short Break Market,* International Journal of Contemporary Hospitality Management, Vol. 9, No. 2, 1997, pp. 55-59.

Farrell K. & Whelan-Ryan F., *Yield Management – A Model for Implementation*, Progress in Tourism and Hospitality Research, No.4, 1998, pp. 267-277.

Fitzsimmons J.A. & Fitzsimmons M. J., *Service Management: Operations, Strategy and Information Technology*, 2nd Edition McGraw-Hill International Editions, Singapore, 1998.

Gamble P. R., *Building a Yield Management System – The Flip Side,* Hospitality Research Journal, 1991, pp. 11-21.

Hansen C. N. & Eringa K., *Critical Success Factors in Yield Management: A Development and Analysis*, Progress in Tourism and Hospitality Research, No.4, 1998, pp. 229-244.

Harris K. J., *Training Technology in the Hospitality Industry: A Matter of Effectiveness and Efficiency,* International Journal of Contemporary Hospitality Management, Vol.7, No.6, 1995, pp. 24-29.

Hoseason J., *Capacity Matters: Yield Management in the Cruise Industry*, in McCasky, D. (Ed) A profitable Partnership Between Industry and Academia, Proceedings of the 4th Annual International Yield and Revenue Management Conference, 1999.

Hott D., Shaw M. & Nusbaum E. F., *Measuring the Effectiveness of an AI/Expert Yield Management System*, The Hospitality Research Journal, 1989, pp. 343-349.

Huyton J. R. & Peters S. D., *Application of Yield Management in the Hotel Industry*, in Yeoman, I. And Ingold, A. (Eds) Yield Management – Strategies for the Service Industries, Cassell, 1997.

Jarvis N., Lindh A. & Jones P., *An Investigation of the Key Criteria Affecting the Adoption of Yield Management in UK Hotels*, Progress in Hospitality and Tourism Research, Vol.4, No.3, 1998, pp. 207-216.

Jauncey S., Mitchell I. & Slamet P., *The Meaning and Management of Yield in Hotels*, International Journal of Contemporary Hospitality Management, Vol.7, No.4, 1995, pp. 23-26.

Jauncey S., Mitchell I., Thompson G. & Specht, F., *Yield Management System Development and Implementation: A Hotel Case Study*, in McCasky, D. (Ed) A profitable Partnership Between Industry and Academia, Proceedings of the 4th Annual International Yield and Revenue Management Conference, 1999.

Jones P. & Hamilton D., *Yield Management: Putting People in the Big Picture*, The Cornell Hotel and Restaurant Administration Quarterly, February, 1992, pp. 89-95.

Kimes S.E., *The Basics of Yield Management*, The Cornell Hotel and Restaurant Administration Quarterly, November, 1989, pp. 14-19.

Lee-Ross D. and Johns,N., *Yield Management in Hospitality SMEs*, International Journal of Contemporary Hospitality Management, Vol.9, No.2, 1997, pp. 66-69.

Leiberman W.H., *Debunking the Myths of Yield Management*, The Cornell Hotel and Restaurant Administration Quarterly, 1993, pp. 34-41.

Luciani, S., *Implementing Yield Management in Small and Medium Sized Hotels: An Investigation of Obstacles and Success Factors in Florence Hotels*, International Journal of Hospitality Management, Vol.9, 1999, pp. 129-142.

MacVicar A. & Rodger J., *Computerised Yield management Systems: A Comparative Analysis of the Human Resource Management Implications*, International Journal of Hospitality Management, Vol.15, No.4, 1996, pp. 325-332.

Noone B. & Andrews N., *The Impact of the Internet on Yield Management Practices in Small and Medium Sized Hospitality Organisations*, in McCasky, D. (Ed) A profitable Partnership Between Industry and Academia, Proceedings of the 4th Annual International Yield and Revenue Management Conference, 1999.

Okumus F. & Hemmington N., *Barriers and Resistance to Change in Hotel Firms: An Investigation at Unit Level*, International Journal of Contemporary Hospitality Management, Vol.10, No.7, 1998, pp. 283-288.

Orkin E., *Boosting Your Bottom Line With Yield Management*, The Cornell HRA Quarterly, February, 1998, pp. 52-56.

Peters S. & Riley J., *Yield Management Transition: A Case Example*, International Journal of Contemporary Hospitality Management, Vol.9, No.2/3, 1997, pp. 89-91.

Rowe M., *Yield Management: Technology Has Opened Up Exciting New Possibilities for a Time-honoured Practice*, Lodging Hospitality February, 1989, pp. 65-66.

TIMS, TIMS Revenue Optimisation Systems, *Installation Agendas,* September 1998a.

TIMS, IMS Revenue Optimisation Systems – press release, *Forte announces the rollout of Optims Yield Management System for the Meridien Brand*, September, 1998b.

Yeoman I. & Watson S., *Yield Management: A Human Activity System,* International Journal of Contemporary Hospitality Management, Vol.9, No.2, 1997, pp. 80-83.

Yin R. K., *Case Study Research – Design and Methods,* (2nd Edition), Sage, 1994.

# Yield Management and trust: the effect of variable pricing on consumer trust in a restaurant brand

## Una McMahon Beattie

Faculty of Business and Management
University of Ulster
Shore Road
Jordanstown
Co. Antrim
Northern Ireland, BT37 0QB


## Adrian Palmer

Professor of Services Marketing
Gloucestershire Business School
Pallas, PO Box 220
The Park Campus
Cheltenham
Gloucestershire, UK, GL50 2QF
United Kingdom


## Patrick McCole

School of Business / Department of Marketing
University of Otago
P.O. Box 56
Dunedin
New Zealand


## Anthony Ingold
Chandelle Consultancy
43 Carlyle Road
Edgbaston, Birmingham, B16 9BH
United Kingdom

# 1   Introduction

Information technology is allowing services organisations to set their prices in very much the same way as traditionally practised in eastern bazaars - by individual bargaining and haggling. "The price list" is not typical of small businesses dealing with small numbers of buyers. It has no part in the business methods of traders in many eastern countries for whom bartering on a one-to-one basis is the norm. Price lists emerged in response to the industrialisation of economies and the growth in the size of markets served by individual firms. Price lists became a method of simplifying transactions between a large organisation and large numbers of its customers.

Over time, there has been a tendency for societies to fragment in their motivations to make purchases, which has been reflected in companies developing increasingly fine methods of segmenting markets (Kotler et al., 1996). In the move from mass marketing to target marketing, firms subtly developed multiple price lists, based on slightly differentiated product offers aimed at different market segments. Today, the process of market segmentation has proceeded to the point where companies can realistically deal with individual market segments (Peppers and Rogers, 1995).

Intriguingly, the conditions for pricing by suppliers of consumer goods and services would appear to be reverting to those which apply in eastern bazaars, in which the seller seeks to apply a price which is uniquely appropriate to each individual buyer. There is plenty of evidence of this move towards unique one-to-one pricing in the Internet based auction sites which have grown in number during the late 1990s (Wisse, 1999, Palmer and McCole, 1999).

On-line auctions represent an extreme case of one-to-one pricing which is being facilitated by information technology. Much more pervasive is the ability of firms to subtly adjust prices offered to individual customers. Rather than having a fixed price list, an enquirer for a specified product may receive different quotations at different times of enquiry. Similarly, two different enquirers may simultaneously receive different price quotations.

The theory and practice of relationship marketing has been based on an assumption that companies are able and willing to enter a dialogue through which additional value is generated (Gummesson, 1998). A seller may learn more about the needs and motivations of individual customers and develop product offers that are unique in satisfying those needs. In this dyadic relationship a seller should be able to assess the value which each individual buyer (or potential buyer) puts on its product, and price its offer uniquely. To economists, the supplier would seek to appropriate the consumer surplus which arises as a result of individuals being prepared to pay a price which is higher than a ruling and uniform market price. Likewise, organisations actively practising YM use differential prices and charge customers using the same service at the same time different prices depending on

customer and demand characteristics (Kimes, 2000). Indeed, Donagl
have outlined a 'Yield Segmentation Process' for managers operatin
and state that it adds value to the customer since it affords the provision ᴏ, ᴀ
product or service that more accurately meets the needs of more clearly defined
groups of guests.

There is now considerable evidence of companies who adjust prices according to
the unique circumstances of individual buyers. National newspapers for example,
typically charge low annual subscriptions to encourage uptake among potential
customers, but reduce their discounts as customers show increasing levels of
loyalty. Travel related companies have become sophisticated in finely adjusting
their prices according to their availability of capacity and the travel motivations of
the buyer. However, variable pricing of this nature would appear to undermine a
central thesis of the relationship marketing argument, that trust is an essential
antecedent of successful long-term buyer-seller relationships (Ganesan 1994;
Morgan and Hunt 1994).

It has been noted that trust is a particularly important factor early in a relationship
and an essential precondition for the relationship to move to more committed
stages of development (Dwyer, Schurr, and Oh 1987; Grayson and Ambler 1999).
YM is essentially a form of price discrimination. Kimes (1994) raised the issue of
customer perception of price variability stating that 'customers must view [new]
procedures and policies as fair'. Therefore, the challenge for the manager
operating a YM system is to maintain the trust of his/her customers.

It is a hypothesis of this research that trust may be undermined where a buyer of
consumer goods or services perceives that the price that they are being offered for
a specified product is less equitable than a similar bundle of benefits offered to
another buyer, or offered to that customer on a different occasion.

The effect of price discrimination on buyer-seller relationships within YM systems
has yet to be explored in research. Similarly, relationship marketing has been
presented as an emerging paradigm during the 1990s, but its underlying axioms
have been increasingly challenged (Saren and Tzokas 1998). This paper explores a
further possible limitation of relationship marketing paradigm and YM systems,
namely that individual price discrimination may be perceived by buyers as
undermining trust in a service provider, and thereby undermining the
sustainability of a relationship.

# 2    Reasons underlying variable pricing

There is considerable evidence of a lack of sophistication in pricing used within
the services sector, with a suggestion that various forms of cost-based pricing
predominate (Zeithaml et al 1985). A company which charges a uniform price for

its products will only achieve maximum possible profits through this pricing method where consumers' evaluation of the product offer is homogenous and there is no consumer surplus. Schematically, companies seek to move from the position in Figure 1a to that in Figure 1b [3].

Fig 1a: Non price discrimination                    Fig 1b: 1st level price discrimination

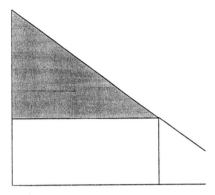

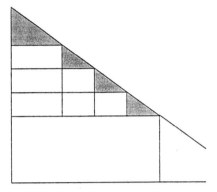

Fig 1a                                                              Fig 1b

Classical micro-economics has been based on an assumption of perfect knowledge within a market place (Lipsey 1996), such that price differences between individuals would become transparent and those buyers who were charged higher prices by one seller would migrate towards sellers offering lower prices. Over time, models of imperfect competition have developed to partially overcome this effect, by recognising that product differentiation produces a number of sub-segments in a market which can be discriminated with differential bundles of product / price offers.

Traditional haggling over prices in open markets was visible for all to see. With modern IT based systems of individual pricing, the results are less visible and can typically only be compared indirectly. The lack of openness in pricing creates conditions for mistrust. Indeed, several recent pricing studies suggest that consumers' reactions to a price change depend not just on the magnitude and direction of the change, but on buyers' perceptions of the seller's circumstances and motivations that led to it (Bobinski et al., 1996). For example, both Kahneman, Knetsch and Thaler (1986) and Kalapurakal, Dickson and Urbany (1991) examined how consumers' perceptions of the "fairness" of price increases were influenced by the circumstances that led to them. Kahneman et al. found that buyers typically perceive a given price increase as "fair" if it is a reaction to an increase in seller costs, but as unfair if it is a reaction to increased consumer demand.

---

[3] Pigou A. C., The economics of welfare, 1920

Similarly, Lichtenstein, Burton and O'Hara (1989) examined how consumers' attributions regarding a retailer's motives for discounting a product influenced their attitudes toward the deal. They found, for example, that consumers had more negative attitudes toward the deal when they attributed it to the retailer's desire to unload a difficult-to-sell offering.

Customer perception is therefore important, especially in relation to the use of IT, since there is a greater opportunity to offer price differentials to consumers on a one-to-one basis. Trust and mistrust are at bi-polar opposites (Pearce, 1974), and consumers' who perceive that suppliers' are untrustworthy through various pricing differentials consider them to be practising malfeasance, and not having their best interests at heart. Therefore, consumers' risk that the price they pay at a particular moment in time is the best price that they will get. Trust and risk are often used interchangeably in the marketing literature.

Williamsom (1993) states that trust in fact is redundant and it can be misleading to use the term trust to describe commercial exchange for which cost-effective safeguards have been devised in support for more efficient exchange. Calculative trust therefore is a contradiction in terms, with a suggestion that consumers conform to theories of economics, with price and not trust, as the focal point for commercial transactions.

Two recent marketing phenomena, assisted by developments in IT, have been particularly important contributors to the development of individual pricing: YM and relationship marketing.

# 3   Individual pricing and relationship marketing

Although the concept of relationship marketing has been positioned at various points between being a short-term tactic and a fundamental marketing philosophy (Fisk, Brown and Bitner, 1993), its core feature is the existence of an ongoing dialogue between partners, such that a buyer will return to a seller in a non-random manner. Repeated purchases from a seller may be the result of a buyer perceiving lower transaction costs in dealing with a previous exchange partner, manifested through simplification of re-ordering processes and a reduction in perceived risk. It has been noted that many ongoing relationships occur as a result of inertia, one explanation of which may be the psychological cost to a buyer which switching suppliers would entail. Ongoing buyer-seller relationships may exist alongside a code of conduct (presumed or formalised) in which a seller is presumed to be acting in co-operation rather than in conflict with the buyer (Luhmann, 1979; Granovetter, 1985; Anderson et al, 1987; Dwyer et al, 1987; Crosby et al, 1990; Miles and Snow, 1992).

# 4 Yield management

In many service sectors, the development of relationship marketing strategies has been developed alongside yield management methods. Yield Management has gained widespread acceptance in number of service industries where it assists the manager to profitably match variable demand with fixed capacity. (Kimes, 1997, 2000, McMahon-Beattie and Palmer, 2000).

Simply, it is a revenue maximisation technique which aims to increase net yield though the predicted allocation of available capacity to predetermined market segments at optimum price (Donaghy et al, 1995). Yield management is not a computer system or a software package but IT has allowed the extensive accumulation, manipulation and analysis of data for effective pricing strategies in forecasted periods of high and low demand. This in effect results in different prices for different people at different times. It is the reason why some airline passengers end up with a better deal than the businessperson who booked his/her flight at the last minute. Again, this highlights the issue of maintaining consumer trust when companies use variable pricing strategies.

Trust is at the heart of relationship marketing and yield management. It is a fundamental element to relational exchange. It is also reasonable to assume that trust is related to equity. Can a buyer trust a seller when there is a suspicion that the seller is providing a lower price to other buyers for an identical bundle of benefits? Likewise, if a new customer is targeted and is rewarded with low prices, what does this say about loyal customers' trust in the supplier? Should it encourage individual buyers to disloyalty?

# 5 Hypothesis of the research

Consumers' level of trust in a company is greater where a policy of uniform pricing is applied, compared with one where prices are flexible in response to supply/demand conditions.

## 5.1 Methodology

The hypothesis is to be tested using a quasi-experimental framework in which a sample of consumers received a series of communications from two organisations for a similar product (a dining club). The two organisations' offers differ only in respect of the method of pricing employed. A longitudinal survey will be conducted in which the series of messages will be communicated to potential and actual customers of the product, differentiated only by price and conditions of availability. Trust by respondents in each product will be measured at the conclusion of the research. The product will be "new" to respondents, so it was assumed that trust at the outset was equal for the two products.

Trust is the dependent variable of this research. Butler (1991) developed a conditions of trust inventory, and these scales were used to measure the conditions of trust in a specific person. For the present study, these scales will be adapted to examine the effects of price discrimination on trust in buyer seller relationships. Butler's scales have been developed from the work of Jennings (1971) and Gabarro (1978) and have been tested for validation and standardisation in many studies. Butler identified 10 conditions of trust 1) availability 2) competence 3) consistency 4) discreteness 5) fairness 6) integrity 7) loyalty 8) openness 9) promise fulfilment, and 10) receptivity. He also developed an eleventh scale 'overall trust', which tests the relationships between the conditions and overall trust in an individual. Butler's scales will be adapted for this study on the basis of the inputs of focus groups. Basic demographic and behavioural variables will also be recorded and analysed. The research will focus on two dining clubs, which offer a similar product in a selection of known restaurants. The dining clubs will be positioned as offering a discount to the normal prices charged by the sample of restaurants. The mean discount will be pitched at 10% below normal prices. However, the dining clubs will differ in their variation of prices around this mean. The sample of consumers will be contacted as follows:

Dining Club A: weekly newsletter by e-mail reminding customers of restaurants. The same discounted prices will be offered at all times.

Dining Club B: weekly newsletter by e-mail giving special offers for the sample of restaurants. Some deep discounts will be offered. At other times the price will be higher than what would have been obtainable by dealing directly with the restaurant.

Dining Club C: as dining club A, but communication was by printed flyer

Dining club D: as dining club B, but communication was by printed flyer.

Each dining club will be given a distinctive name to improve memorability. Six iterations will follow over a period of 6 weeks. Respondents will have personal knowledge of the restaurants involved. The limitations of this approach are recognised. The research cannot develop trust on the basis of tangible property qualities since there were no actual interaction with the service on which trust could be based. However, the research design will allow trust to focus on messages and how these are manipulated. By assumption, all of the dining clubs will be equal in their ability to deliver what is promised.

# 6   Conclusions and management implications

By the nature of longitudinal research, it will take some time to gather in all data and to analyse it for the development of trust. Too much research on the subjects of trust and relationship marketing has relied on cross-sectional data and, as yet, no research has been carried out on the effect of variable pricing on the level of consumer trust in YM. As such the results of this research should provide service managers with more customer-orientated YM strategies and ultimately improve the effectiveness of their YM systems. Despite the advantages of the approach adopted here, its limitation should be recognised, especially the absence of a significant level of risk on the part of participants.

# References

Anderson E., Lodish L.M. & Weitz B.A., *Resource Allocation Behaviour in Conventional Channels*, Journal of Marketing Research, 24 (February), 1987, pp 85-97.

Butler J.K., *Toward Understanding and Measuring Conditions of Trust: Evolution of a Conditions of Trust Inventory*, Journal of Management, 17 (3), 1991, pp 643-663

Crosby L.A., Evans K.R., & Cowles D., *Relationship Quality in Services Selling: An Interpersonal Influence Perspective,* Journal of Marketing, 54 (July), 1990, pp.68-81

Donaghy K. McMahon U & McDowell, D., *Yield Management: An Overview*, International Journal of Hospitality Management, 14 (2), 1995, pp 139-150

Donaghy K., McMahon-Beattie U., Yeoman,I. & Ingold A., *The Realism of Yield Management*, Progress in Tourism and Hospitality Research, 4, 1998, pp 187-195

Dwyer F. Robert, Paul H. Schurr & Sejo Oh, *Developing Buyer-Seller Relationships*, Journal of Marketing, 51 (April), 1987, pp 11-27.

Fisk R.P., S.W. Brown & M.J. Bitner, *Tracking the Evolution of the Services Marketing Literature*, Journal of Retailing, 69 (1), 1993, pp 61-103

Ganesan & Shankar (), *Determinants of Long-Term Orientation in Buyer-Seller Relationships*, Journal of Marketing, 58 (April), 1994, pp 1-19.

Granovetter M., *Economic Action and Social Structure: The Problem of Emdeddedness*, American Journal of Sociology, Vol. 91, 1985, pp. 481-510

Grayson, Kent and Tim Ambler, *The dark side of long-term relationships in marketing services*, Journal of Marketing Research, 36 (1 ), 1999, p 132

Gummesson E., *Implementation Requires a Relationship Marketing Paradigm,* Academy of Marketing Science, 26(3), 1998, pp. 242-249

Kahneman D., Knetsch J. & Thaler R., *Fairness as a Constraint on Profit Seeking: Entitlements in the Market*, The American Economic Review, 76 (September), 1986, pp 728-741.

Kalapurakal R., Dickson P. & Urbany. J., *Perceived Price Fairness and Dual Entitlement*, 1991, pp. 788-793 in Rebecca Holman and Michael Solomon (eds.), *Advances in Consumer Research*, 18. Provo, UT: Association for Consumer Research

Kimes S., *Yield Management: An Overview, in Yeoman, I and Ingold*, A. (Eds) Yield Management, Strategies for the Service Industries, London, Cassell, 1997, pp 3-11.

Kimes S, *A Strategic approach to Yield Management, in Ingold*, A., McMahon-Beattie, U., and Yeoman, I. (Eds) Yield Management, Strategies for the Service Industries, 2nd edition, London, Continuum, Forthcoming, 2000.

Kotler P., Makens J. & Bowens J., *Marketing for Hospitality and Tourism,* New Jersey: Prentice-Hall, 1996.

Lichtenstein D., Burton S. &. O'Hara. B.S., *Marketplace Attributions and Consumer Evaluations of Discount Claims*, Psychology and Marketing, 6 (Fall), 1989, pp. 163-180.

Lipsey R.G., *Microeconomics,* Addison Wesley Longman, 1996.

Luhmann, N., *Trust and Power*, New York: John Wiley, 1979.

McMahon-Beattie U & Palmer A., *One for All or All for One: A Comparison of Everyday Low Pricing and Yield Management Strategies in the Hotel Industry,* Journal of Targeting, Measurement and Analysis for Marketing, 8 (3), 2000, pp. 249-258.

Miles R.E. & Snow C.C., *Causes of Failure in Network Organisations*, California Management Review, Summer, 1992, pp.93-72.

Morgan, Robert M. & Shelby D. Hunt, *The Commitment-Trust Theory of Relationship Marketing*, Journal of Marketing, 58 (July), 1994, pp. 20-38.

Palmer A. & McCole P., *The Virtual Re-intermediation of travel Services: A Conceptual Framework and Empirical Investigation*, Journal of Vacation Marketing, 6 (1), 1999, pp.33-47.

Pearce W.B., *Trust and Interpersonal Communication*, Speech Monographs, 41, 1974, pp. 236-244.

Pigou A. C., *The economics of welfare*, 1920.

Saren M.J. & Tzokas, *Some dangerous axioms of relationship marketing*, Journal of Strategic Marketing; 6 ( 3), 1998.

Peppers D. & Rogers M., *A New Paradigm: Share of Customer, Not Market Share*, 5 (3), 1995, pp. 48-51.

Williamson, O.E., *Calculativeness, Trust, and Economic Organisation*, Journal of Law and Economics, 36, 1993, pp. 453-486.

Wisse B., *The Internet- The Future of Travel Distribution*, Key Note Speaker at the 1999 European Travel and Tourism Research Association Conference, Dublin, Ireland, 1999. http://www.trc.dit.ie/priceline.ppt

Zeithaml V.A., Parasuraman A. & Berry L.L., *Problems and Strategies in Services Marketing*, Journal of Marketing, 49, Spring, 1985, pp. 33-46.

# Controlling the yield management process in the hospitality business

**Paolo Desinano, Maria Stella Minuti, Emanuela Schiaffella**

Università di Perugia, Facoltà di Economia

Centro Italiano di Studi Superiori sul Turismo e sulla Promozione Turistica
Via C.Cecci, 1
06088 S.M. degli Angeli, Assisi (PG).
Italy.

*Contents: 1 Introduction. 2 A general framework to control hotel YMS. 3 General considerations about demand forecasting. 4 General considerations about room inventory control. 5 The control process: tracking. 5.1 Inventory report. 5.2 Sales report. 5.3 Reservation report. 5.4 Pricing report. 5.5 Unsold report. 6 The control process: checking. 7 The control process: signalling. 8 The control process: controlling and updating. 9 Conclusions. References*

## 1 Introduction

This paper focuses on the control activities entailed within a Yield Management (YM) system for the hospitality business. The technical literature on this issue is rather rare despite the fact that this topic is very critical in the evaluation of the business effectiveness of the whole YM process.

Our intention in this introduction is to define the meanings of "YM system" and of "control" to avoid possible misunderstandings. Our framework is based on the following assumptions:

1. We agree with the YM system definition contained in EC report (European Commission, 1997). Precisely, we think that an authentic YM system corresponds to those classified as "very high" in the report cited above.

2. The generic conceptual framework of a YM system is organised into five main function components: market segmentation, pricing, forecasting, inventory management and reservation.

3. The general criterion for managing the YM system is the concept of bid-price.

4. The control regards a single-unit firm. We have not considered the case of multiple-unit firms such as hotel chains, consortia, et cetera.

5. The control illustrated considers neither organisational nor marketing aspects and is limited to investigating the effectiveness of the demand forecasting process.

In this paper our intention is to organise the many suggestions that have emerged from studies and common practice in regard to the control issues of YMS into a systematic framework.

In a YM oriented approach, systematic control is fundamental for (Educational Institute of the American Hotel & Motel Association, 1990; Orkin E. B., 1988):

1. judging the effectiveness of forecasts;

2. measuring the adequacy of YM systems and procedures;

3. monitoring denials/regrets and confirmations for measuring the economic performance.

It is also important for assessing the performance of individuals and departments in their efforts to achieve yield objectives [1] (for example, it may be important to measure daily average revenue associated with a particular booking agent, in relation to daily revenue potentially obtainable by the agent; and for observing the impact of YM oriented strategies and tactics, leading to optimisation of their application (Orkin, 1988).

The paper is organised into a section describing the general control architecture and, after some general considerations about forecasting and room inventory control, in four subsequent sections that treat specific issues regarding the phases in which the control process can be articulated. A final section summarises the topics discussed.

## 2   A general framework to control hotel YMS

This paragraph illustrates one possible general framework we can use to classify and place the various activities entailed. The framework is based on the following considerations. Within the global control activity, we can make a distinction among tracking, checking, signalling and "control" in the strict sense of the word. The controls are based on the data produced by hotel sales.

Then the first key component of an effective control system is a sales tracking system that collects and organises the data generated during sale transactions.

---

[1]   A timely training programme for developing a working knowledge of the YM system and for motivating employees towards yield objectives is very important. An interesting work on this topic in the implementation phase is in (Donaghy, McMahon Beattie and McDowell, 1997).

From this control phase, information reports are periodically and regularly issued. They contain records of the actual values of different parameters regarding reservation and sales patterns.

The second key component of the control process is a checking system that compares the data tracked with parameters set by the yield manager. The output of this comparison are two types of reports: warning reports and fatal reports, the former evidence slight anomalies while the latter report critical situations for the YMS. We called this activity of notification "signalling". These reports feed control activity in the strict sense. Tracking, checking and signalling can be performed by software while the yield analyst performs the control.

Figure 1: This figure illustrates the overall control process.

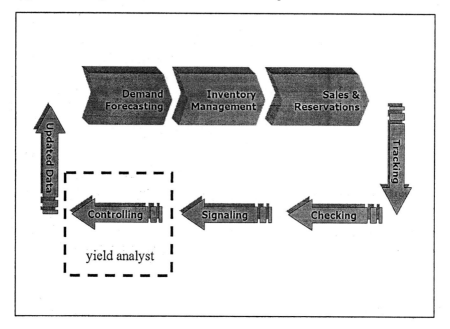

# 3  General considerations about demand forecasting

The importance of demand forecasting in the YM system has been greatly stressed because forecasts represent the building blocks for optimisation and for room inventory management (Kimes, 1989).

Therefore the accuracy of forecasts is of special importance because the effectiveness of the whole YM system is derived from it. Consequently, monitoring the accuracy of forecasts is an important part of the hotel YM system control process. The problem of forecast accuracy concerns two different issues:

the first one can be seen as an *ex ante* problem regarding the measures a model must adopt for a high level of accuracy. The second one can be seen as an *ex post* problem and regards the evaluation of forecast accuracy by comparing the forecast values with the actual values, that is, the real forecasting control process.

With regard to the *ex ante* issue, there are several factors, which can determine the accuracy of the forecasts (Cross, 1997; Curry, 1994; Granger, 1989):

- the forecasts must be carried out for different customer segments as booking patterns, perception of the product and willingness to pay vary from segment to segment;

- the data set used for the forecast model must be the largest and most accurate possible: if the input data used as explanatory variables are inaccurate then the forecast will be inaccurate too and generally more data means more accurate forecasts;

- forecasts must be updated frequently: because most of the demand forecasting models[2] rely on reservations on hand at various dates before the date of stay, as the hotel receives new reservations these must be added to the model and the model must be carried out again. As (Cross, 1997) says:

  "there are three secrets to accurately forecasting the behaviour of nonconformist consumers in the amoeba market: reforecast, reforecast, reforecast. Things happen every day that destroy the accuracy of your forecast, no matter how much data you use or how accurate your forecasting methodology is. The only way to keep up with the increasingly entropic market is through reviewing, reassessing, and reforecasting."

YM operates on a daily basis: decisions on allocations must be made for individual future days and for this reason forecasting models provide daily forecasts of future demand. Therefore at least a daily updating of the forecast is required for good model performance and, in fact, many hotels update their forecasts every day. But sometimes, if the hotel has high levels of activity, more frequent updating, for example every hour or even less, is required. Some hotels update their forecasts even after each customer transaction.

Forecast updating is necessary to improve the accuracy of the model but it is not sufficient to guarantee its complete effectiveness.

In fact, despite the considerable amount of information that is continuously added to the reservation database, it is necessary to frequently monitor the adequacy of the model in use and, if necessary, re-calibrate the model parameters (Schwartz and Hiemstra, 1997). These issues, as they are related to the various phases of the real control process, will be discussed in their respective paragraphs.

---

[2] A list of forecasting methods and models is given in (Desinano, Minuti, Schiaffella, Sfodera, 1999).

# 4 General considerations about room inventory control

In hotel YMS control it is important to focus on four aspects: definition and allocation of room inventory, length-of-stay control and group booking. Reports should be available to the yield analyst allowing the manipulation of a given room inventory structure when market conditions change.

The capacity definition must be determined in view of offsetting the effects of cancellations, of no-shows and of early check outs, projected between the control date and the arrival date. In this way, by allowing for inventory overbooking, hotels attempt to minimise the spoilage situation, whenever a unit of capacity is allowed to go unsold (Wheatherford, 1991).

In an imprudent configuration, it is possible to define the overbooking level within a local market structure, where nearby competing properties can solve any overselling problem. Furthermore, the possibility of up-grading allows for a more aggressive overbooking policy.

The allocation process requires a nested inventory structure, based on buckets of various parameters, for example length of stay, different packages and so on (Berretta, Desinano, Minuti, Schiaffella and Sfodera, 2000). There are many optimisation techniques for the protection of each bucket, based on a mathematical programming approach or on a marginal revenue heuristic (Yeoman and Ingold, 1997), but the objective is to limit sales in the lower value classes and encourage up-sells. Since hotels offer several products or packages, a multi-dimensional inventory nesting structure (Desinano, Minuti, Schiaffella and Sfodera, 1999) is more appropriate.

The length of stay control process trades off one and/or multiple day requests, given displaced revenues generated by accept/deny decisions.

Another important component of the hotel YM toolbox is the control of group bookings, taking into account the expected spilled demand [3], the expected displaced revenue and the expected relocated demand (walk-in guests) [4].

---

[3] When full price demand is denied for at least one discount customer, it is spill. (Wheatherford, 1991).
[4] See on this argument (Bastiani, 1999).

# 5 The control process: tracking

As we have said, the first key component of an effective control system is a sales tracking system that collects and organises the data generated during sale transactions.

The data tracked can be organised in output reports [5], by information objective, issued periodically and regularly (Figure 2).

Some examples of these reports are listed below.

Figure 2: Type of reports issued in control process phases

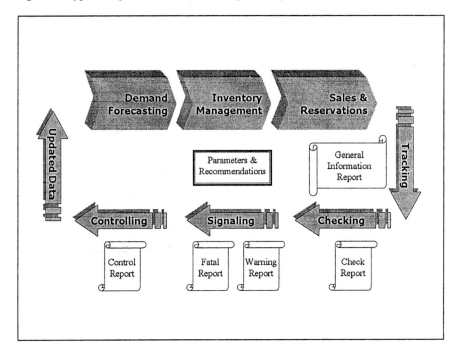

## 5.1 Inventory report

This report illustrates the room inventory situation, referred to a given time frame (for example one or two weeks). So, one could visualise, line by line:

– arrival date;

– day of week;

---

[5]  A good illustration of Optims software reports is in (Pizzolante, 1999).

- days remaining to arrival date;

- rooms available;

- actual level of overbooking;

- actual level of acceptable reservations for each rate class (if nesting structure is adopted).

## 5.2  Sales report

This report illustrates various information about room sales and can be issued daily, weekly and monthly. Line by line, this report, concerning a given arrival date, could contain (all data are recorded by rate class):

- actual rooms sold, by length of stay;

- actual rooms sold to clients arriving on the date;

- actual rooms occupied by stay-overs;

- actual rooms occupied by over-stays;

- actual level of no-shows;

- actual level of early check-outs;

- actual average daily revenue;

- rate percentage (found dividing actual average daily revenue by the rack rate);

- actual number of rooms sold to walk-ins;

- actual extra revenues;

- actual displaced rooms and revenues;

- actual spilled demand;

- group net revenue (that is, actual group revenues minus displaced revenues);

- yield percentage, obtained dividing revenue realised for the specified day by potential revenue for that day;

- actual revenue per available room;

- actual revenue per available customer.

## 5.3  Reservation report

This report contains various information about room reservations and can be issued daily, weekly and monthly.

Line by line, this report, concerning a given arrival date, could contain (all data are recorded by rate class):

-   days remaining to arrival date;
-   actual rooms sold, by length of stay;
-   actual level of turnaways;
-   actual level of definitive reservations;
-   actual level of non-definitive reservations;
-   actual level of reservation with options;
-   actual level of reservation without options;
-   actual level of guaranteed reservation;
-   actual level of non-guaranteed reservation;
-   actual level of denials;
-   actual level of regrets;
-   actual level of no-shows;
-   actual level of cancellations.

## 5.4  Pricing report

This report could contain, for each day, the threshold values (or the bid price [6]) calculated by the YM system. In particular:

-   rate classes deriving from marketing analysis;
-   bid price for the day;
-   length of stay bid price [7];
-   minimum acceptance price [8].

---

[6]   Bid prices are set for the room and the service is sold only if the offered rate exceeds the sum of the bid prices of all units needed to supply the service (Talluri, Van Ryzin, 1998); (EBNT, Ires Liguria, Ial Emilia Romagna, CST Assisi, Accademia CT Trento, 1998).

[7]   In a simplified version, the length of stay bid price is the arithmetical average of the bid prices of different days comprising the period of stay (EBNT, Ires Liguria, Ial Emilia Romagna, CST Assisi, Accademia CT Trento, 1998).

[8]   Minimum price of acceptance is obtained dividing the difference of displaced revenue minus extra-room revenue by the number of requests (Bastiani, 1999).

## 5.5 Unsold report

This report could be referred to a given time frame and could allow the visualisation of some causes that could generate an unsold; in particular, line by line:

- arrival date;
- day of week;
- days remaining to arrival date;
- room capacity available for any arrival date;
- actual level of turnaways;
- actual level of definitive reservations;
- actual level of non definitive reservations;
- actual level of reservation with options;
- actual level of reservation without options;
- actual level of denials;
- actual level of regrets,
- actual level of no-shows;
- actual level of cancellations;
- actual level of over-stay;
- actual level of early check-outs.

# 6 The control process: checking

The second key component of the control activity is checking focused on the comparison between the data tracked and that forecasted (YM systems could also produce recommendation reports, as in figure 2, in which the yield analyst can find information concerning an optimal scenario system, elaborated on the basis of segmentation, forecasting, overbooking and allocation models).

In this phase of control process, check reports (Figure 2) are useful and contain records extrapolated from information reports, issued in the tracking phase, and from forecasting process.

These reports, concerning a given arrival date, could contain (all data are recorded by rate class):

- days remaining to arrival date;
- expected/actual rooms sold, by length of stay;
- expected/actual rooms sold to clients arriving on the date;
- expected/actual rooms occupied by stay-overs;
- expected/actual rooms occupied by over-stays;
- expected/actual level of no-shows;
- expected/actual level of early check-outs;
- expected/actual number of cancellations;
- expected/actual number of rooms sold to walk-ins;
- expected/actual spilled demand;
- expected/actual level of definitive reservations;
- expected/actual level of non definitive reservations;
- expected/actual level of reservation with options;
- expected/actual level of reservation without options.

The evaluation of forecast accuracy is based on the magnitude of the forecast error, that is, on the difference between forecast value and actual value. The selection of the best error measure is not simple because of the absence of a single universally accepted measure of accuracy (Schwartz 1999). The most common measures of accuracy are:

- mean absolute deviation (MAD);
- mean squared error (MSE);
- mean absolute percentage error (MAPE);
- mean square percentage error (MSPE);
- standard deviation of error (SDE) [9].

The selection of an appropriate error measure is, however, an important task since the error measure should reflect the estimated damage caused by the forecast error, i.e. the cost of error (Schwartz, 1999). For example, the squared error measures assume that as the forecast error increases, the resulting damage to the hotel increases exponentially. This is not the case of ratio (percentage) based error

---

[9] A list of the most common measures of accuracy with a detailed report of their use in the literature and the justifications adduced to their choice is given in (Witt and Witt, 1992).

measures which are less affected by extreme errors and, being independent of scale, are good relative measures when comparing different techniques.

Unfortunately there is little empirical evidence of the actual cost of error functions in the hotel industry. It has been said that the cost of an over-forecast error can be approximated by the hotel production cost function which is more often linear than exponential, while the cost of an under-forecast error is more difficult to generalise (Schwartz, 1999).

On the contrary, studies conducted in the airline sector (Curry, 1994) reveal that over-forecasting is more harmful than under-forecasting because it has a greater impact on revenue. The same considerations made for this sector seem applicable to hotels as over-forecasting could save too many rooms and the hotel is more likely to remain with some empty rooms, thus losing the entire amount of the rate, while under-forecasting leads to a full hotel but with too many discount clients (not enough rooms saved for the late-booking, high value client). The loss in this situation is the difference between full and discounted rates.

As we have seen it is quite probable that the cost of the forecast error is asymmetrical; that is, the cost of an over-forecast error might be larger (or smaller) than the cost of an under-forecast error. This asymmetry should be properly addressed by the error measure and (Schwartz, 1999) suggests a cost of error function when over-forecast and under-forecast costs are different.

As we have seen, since the actual cost of error is not known for a certainty, it is not possible to indicate a single error measure that is likely to be more appropriate. In practice, because there is no evidence of a quadratic loss function, preference in many cases goes to MAD and MAPE, also because they facilitate comparison between different forecasting models. This is not a secondary reason as there are many methods applicable for forecasting hotel reservations and often the choice of the most appropriate model can be difficult.

# 7   The control process: signalling

The last formalised phase of the YM control is signalling. The outputs of this phase are two types of reports: warning reports and fatal reports, the former notify slight anomalies while the latter report critical situations for the YMS (Figure 2). As we have already said, once a particular forecasting model has been chosen, a constant monitoring of its adequacy is absolutely necessary for the effectiveness of the entire YM system. Therefore the analysis of error measures is also a tool in the continuous evaluation of the accuracy of forecasts so as to intervene at the first sign of excessive deviation between forecasted and actual data. A very useful tool for the systematic monitoring of forecasting accuracy is the tracking signal and graph (Kimes, 1998). Tracking signal values can be calculated by dividing the cumulative forecast errors by the moving MADs. Tracking signal values generally near zero show a good performance of the forecast model in time, while values far from zero, positive or negative, are signals of poor forecast accuracy deriving from forecasts lower (under-forecast) or higher (over-forecast) than the actual values.

The graph of the tracking signal values over time (i.e. days) offers the best way to analyse the trend of the forecast error as time goes by. As long as the analysis of the graph reveals a tracking signal trend within an acceptable range, forecasts can be considered under control and therefore accurate.

Naturally these range values cannot be defined universally but vary according to specific characteristics of the hotel (Bolt, 1988). A hotel that registers high demand fluctuations from period to period must expect a higher error margin and therefore define a higher tolerance range compared to a hotel that operates in a more stable environment. However an empirical rule has been defined (Kimes, 1998) which indicates that a range lower than $\pm 3\sigma$ can be considered acceptable. If the tracking signal values escape the range of values considered acceptable and if this situation goes on, it is necessary to make some adjustments to the forecast model.

In fact, the control process should not be restricted to an evaluation of the forecast performance compared to actual values, but should help in identifying the reasons for high deviations between forecasted and actual values and consequently point out possible remedies (Bolt, 1988). For example, high tracking signal values, consistently positive or negative, might result from new demand trends: a resort has become a less popular destination or, on the contrary, it attracts more tourists as a result of some event (for example the opening of a new congress centre in the area). In such cases the forecast analyst must consider these new factors, reassessing, i.e. increasing or reducing, the forecasts. Only one or few anomalous values of the tracking signal (very high or low) can instead result from isolated factors, which perhaps are not going to happen again (for example a major sport or cultural event). In this case the anomalous registered value must be realigned because it can invalidate future forecasts (Granger, 1989).

When there are no evident explanations for large differences between forecasted and actual values, the adopted forecasting technique may no longer be adequate and it could be necessary to evaluate alternative forecasting methods.

# 8 The control process: controlling and updating

The control process continues with the control phase, in which the yield analyst evaluates any warning or fatal signals; it is important to emphasise that the human factor in hotel forecasting and control cannot be underestimated (Orkin, 1989).

Forecasts must be carefully evaluated by a manager who knows the market conditions in which his hotel operates.

Therefore the analyst's "clinical judgement" of the surrounding environment must be the last and most important control form available for YM.

The output of this phase is the control report, in which the yield analyst formalises his evaluations and considerations (Figure 2). Finally, there is the analyst's real intervention that may be articulated in two levels: the first concerns access to a model for running simulations; the second level allows the modification of the model and its parameters, for example the number of transient available reservations (Daudel and Vialle, 1989).

# 9   Conclusions

The importance of these control phases within the YM process is straightforward. This paper was not intended to propose any special innovations in hospitality YM practices but to reorder the various controlling options into an organic outline. We think that this outline is useful both for future research and as a practical tool. In fact these reports can be use as check-list to evaluate commercial YM systems or to measure the YM "orientation" of existing hotel information systems.

# References

Bastiani S., *La clientela organizzata in albergo: analisi e gestione nell'ambito di uno Yield Management System*, tesi di laurea, Economia del Turismo, Università di Perugia, 1999.

Pizzolante G., *Le Meridien & Forte - Una catena che applica uno yield management system*, tesi di diploma, Economia e gestione dei servizi turistici, Università di Perugia, 1999.

Bolt G.J., *Market and Sales Forecasting*, Franklin Watts, New York, 1988.

Cross R.G., *Revenue management: hard-core tactics for market domination*, Brodway Books, New York, 1997.

Curry R.E., *Forecasting For Revenue Management, Scorecard – Technical brief*, Third Quarter, 1994.

Desinano P., Minuti M.S., Schiaffella E. & Sfodera F., *Issues regarding yield management application in the hospitality industry. New directions for research*, Proceedings of the 4th Annual International Yield Management Conference, Colchester (UK), 1999.

Berretta M., Desinano P., Minuti M. S., Schiaffella E. & Sfodera F., *Yield Management - Uno strumento innovativo per la gestione dei ricavi nelle imprese turistiche*, Economia & Management, n. 2, Marzo, 2000, p. 73-90.

Donaghy K., McMahon Beattie U. & McDowell D., *Implementing yield management: lessons from the hotel sector*, International Journal of Contemporary Hospitality Management, 9/2, 1997, p. 50-54.

EBNT, Ires Liguria, Ial Emilia Romagna, CST Assisi, Accademia CT Trento, *Yield Management per le piccole e medie imprese ricettive*, software ipertestuale per le Unità Formative Capitalizzabili '98-'99, 1998.

Daudel S. & Vialle G., *Le yield management*, InterEditions, Paris, 1989.

Educational Institute of the American Hotel & Motel Association, *Yield Management – Video Program Companion Materials*, Michigan, 1990.

European Commission, *Yield Management in small and medium-sized enterprises in the tourism industry - General report*, Luxembourg, 1997.

Granger C.W.J., *Forecasting in Business and Economics*, Academic Press, San Diego (CA), 1989.

Kimes S.E., *The basic of Yield Management*, The Cornell H.R.A. Quarterly, November, Vol.30. No.3, 1989, p. 14-19.

Kimes S.E., *Seminar in Yield management*, CST, Assisi, May 18-20, 1998.

Orkin E.B., *Boosting Your Bottom Line with Yield Management*, The Cornell H.R.A. quarterly, February , 1988,.p 52-56

Orkin E.B., *Forecasting: Cristall Ball or CRT? The Bottomline*, June-July, 1989, p. 20-29.Schwartz Z., *Monitoring the accuracy of multiple occupancy forecasts*, FIU Hospitality Review, Vol.17, Nos. 1 & 2, Spring/Fall, 1999, p. 29-42.

Schwartz Z. & Hiemstra S., *Improving the Accuracy of Hotel Reservation Forecasting: Curve Similarity Approach*, Journal of Travel Research, Summer, 1997, p. 3-14.

Talluri K. & Van Ryzin G., *An analysis of bid price controls for network revenue management*, Management Science, vol. 44, no. 11, part 1 of 2, november, 1998, p. 1577-1593.

Wheatherford L. R., *Perishable Asset Revenue Management in General Business Situations,* Ph.D. Dissertation, Darden Graduate School of Business Administration, University of Virginia, 1991.

Witt S.F. & Witt C.A., *Modeling and Forecasting Demand in Tourism*, Academic Press, London, 1992.

Yeoman I. & Ingold A., *Yield Management. Strategies for the Service Industries*, Cassell, London, 1997.

# Part II
# Yield management: new applications

# Revenue management in visitor attractions: a case study of the EcoTech Centre, Swaffham, Norfolk

**Julian Hoseason**

Academic Dean
Institute for Higher Education – Butte Campus
Glion Hotel School
Route de Glion 111
1825 Glion sur Montreux
Switzerland

*Contents: 1 Introduction. 2 Background. 3 The economics of visitor attractions. 4 Marketing and ideal markets. 5 Yield management. 6 Data gathering. 7 Results and discussion. 8 Conclusions. References.*

# 1   Introduction

Visitor attractions form an integral part of the total tourism product for both the domestic and incoming visitors to a region. Attractions cover a broad spectrum of activities based upon the natural or man-made environment ranging from heritage sites through to purpose built centres usually devoted to leisure and recreational activities (Getz, 1993; Swarbrooke, 1999; Hall and Page, 1999).

The attractions sector is complex in definition and provides different levels of engagement with the visitor when the 'encounter' takes place (Crouch, 1999). While visitors enjoy this variety, attractions offer an intangible experience (Yeoman and Leask, 1999) which makes visitor management and marketing complex (Prentice *et al,* 1998*)* since seasonality and a spatial element enters into the pricing strategy.

In the mid 1990s Norfolk was experiencing a decline in its agricultural base and indicators suggested alternative strategies needed implementation to avoid unemployment and social blight in the community of Swaffham. Regional funding from the European Union enabled an imaginative proposal for the development of a sustainable attraction to act as a growth-pole for inward investment.

The EcoTech Centre was to be an experimental showcase in design and construction techniques with the emphasis upon environmental management and education. As an attraction, the EcoTech Centre would need to reach a critical mass of around 50,000 visitors per annum to be viable. The centre would be competing against the region's existing attractions, the coast and an area of wetland known as the 'Norfolk Broads'. Yield Management (YM) is widely regarded as a technique for balancing demand and supply through rigorous management of revenue (Cross, 1998; Edgar, 1998; Farrell and Whelan-Ryan; 1998; Daudel and Vialle, 1994). The success of YM is dependent upon a balanced relationship between inventory or capacity management and pricing strategies (Kimes, 1997; Cross, 1998). To optimize revenue, YM uses mathematical algorithms (Belobaba and Wilson, 1997) to improve profitability. Reduction in seasonal fluctuations in demand produces greater financial stability and in the attractions sector may assist in the conservation of sites where carrying capacities have been reached. YM has been widely adopted by most service industries, especially in airlines (Larsen, 1988; Ingold and Huyton, 1997), hospitality (Orkin, 1988; Donaghy et al; 1995) tour operations (Hoseason and Johns, 1998; Laws, 1997) and in the cruise industry (Dickinson and Vladimir, 1997; Cross, 1998) and is now widely accepted as part of strategic management.

As the implementation of YM matures across the travel and tourism industry, the attractions sector has yet to extensively adopt YM as a management technique that produces lower financial performance in comparison to other sectors. Research by Yeoman and Leask (1999) into heritage visitor attractions indicated the highly seasonal nature of the market necessitated in revenue management techniques being applied to main season activities with more specialist activities being introduced during low or out of season periods for maximization in revenue. However, major capital projects funded by the UK's National Lottery, may have caused distortion to the attractions sector at local, regional and national level where sudden increases in market capacity cannot be met by corresponding increases in visitor activity.

Over £1.2 billion has been awarded to over 180 major projects with an additional £2.8 billion being awarded through European funded grants for projects (Anon, 2000). Key projects like the Royal Armouries in Leeds, or, the Earth Centre have failed to live up to projections not only visitor numbers, but also in revenue management where over-estimates and losses threaten their future (McClarence, 2000). For the EcoTech Centre, its future success may not simply lie in developing a highly innovative attraction, but consider micro-market behaviour in relation to the capacity of the 'ideal market' or catchment area.

# 2   Background

The EcoTech Centre has been built on a brown-field site on the edge of

Swaffham, a market town in the centre of Norfolk. Sited on a former derelict firework factory, the project aimed at cleaning up a polluted site for the benefit of the community. The original proposal envisaged an experimental building in design and construction techniques attracting 50,000 visitors pa and provides an interactive learning centre based on environmental education. By targeting the enhancement of leisure and tourism facilities, it was hoped to attract high inward investment to a showcase project.

Regeneration would provide a high profile attraction in order to bolster the regional tourism and leisure product base. An experimental building would provide an opportunity to be innovative in not only design, but also construction techniques where fusion between designers and the construction industry could present alternatives to current building practices where visitors and the community would be engaged with the project.

The 'environmentally friendly' experimental building was designed to embrace energy efficiency, ecological waste treatment and provide a centre for environmental education with facilities in skills training for the local community. Management and marketing of a multi-faceted project requires great understanding of site development and management where market segment behaviour and pricing strategies for the management of revenue are effectively implemented.

The EcoTech Centre would form part of an economic growth pole (Higgins, 1983) where a group of 'propulsive enterprises' would produce spread effects within the region. d'Hauteserre (1997) highlighted the positive economic impacts this technique brought to the Marne Valley since the establishment of Disneyland, Paris.

The EcoTech Centre was planned by the partnership between Breckland District Council and the EcoTech Centre Trustees to be a high profile EU funded capital project to optimize benefits to the community. Offering an eco - based experience would attract additional investment into the region and alter the publics' perceptions of the attractions sector profile.

Provision of a sustainable resource was seen as critical to the project. As part of the site development programme, a wind turbine with viewing platform was built by Ecotricity and opened to visitors in May 1999. Instantly, this massive structure provided a focal point and Unique Selling Point (USP) for the site since there were no similar attractions in the UK. The decision to construct a viewing platform had been based upon visitor experiences of a similar attraction in Europe.

The opening of the wind turbine has pushed visitor numbers up to 28,500 and revised targets have been reduced to 32,000 which reflects current performance more accurately.

Future plans include the development of an experimental eco-house, organic garden and using COPIS funding, build an interactive walk-through compositor to enhance the attractions coverage of future techniques in sustainability of resources. As EcoTech matures as an attraction and the novelty factor diminishes the need for revenue management will increase. The reliance upon re-designing of interpretation and programmes of exhibitions will form only part of the revenue management strategy where the shift towards more specialist and community-based micro-markets will need to be addressed.

# 3    The economics of visitor attractions

The visitor attractions sector is highly fragmented and diverse (Bull, 1995). The very diversity in nature of the market dictates the economic conditions which impact upon the market and the operators or suppliers within in it. At one end of the product continuum natural heritage sites are often free to visitors and managed either by government agencies, for example English Heritage or organisations like the National Trust that has charity status.

At the other end of the continuum, there are commercially based organisations providing built attractions that require profit or revenue maximization (Bull, 1995;Tribe, 1995; Yeoman and Leask, 1999). Since alteration to public funding in the 1990s, many organisations irrespective of organisational structure and status, have increasingly used commercial i.e. revenue maximization techniques to support attractions' viability. Similar to the accommodation sector, visitor attractions (Yeoman and Leask, 1999) are capital intensive or are high in capital value as in the case of built heritage sites. However, there is also an 'unpriced' value (Bull, 1995) within the economic structure of attractions.

These include social cost/ benefit pricing and tourist values that are elements all included within the tourist product. They may be inseparable from the experience, but cannot be given a market value (Sinden and Worrell, 1979) and this particularly applies to the natural environment. Managers of visitor attractions subsequently manage revenue through either profit maximization, break-even pricing or social cost/ benefit pricing.

As Bull (1995) points out, it makes comparison of economic or financial performance almost impossible, particularly where local authority assist in financial support or donations are made. A number of high profile projects funded through the National Lottery, for example, the Millennium Dome or the Armouries in Sheffield, have foundered where altruism and social cost/ benefit pricing has tried to defy gravity models along with economic modelling in demand and supply. The result: a distorted picture in terms of visitor numbers and ultimately the financial viability. A massive influx in major projects funded by the National Lottery has caused existing attractions management problems on national, regional and local scales.

Wanhill (1998) identified attractions have high fixed costs either through capital investment required to establish or to expand the development of an attraction. Operational and variable costs are impacted upon by the seasonality of the attraction and may force operators to use cost-orientated pricing to ensure contribution margins are met. While admissions prices form the core of income generation (Swarbrooke, 1999), each attraction suffers from an element of price discretion to cover short run operational costs (Bull, 1995; Wanhill, 1998). Low marginal costs may enable a greater range in price discretion. However, pricing strategies often include an element of visitor's perception of 'value for money'. Reliance on measuring admission prices based upon a general rule of market knowledge and visitor perception increases risk. High visitor numbers are usually required to meet break-even points and this makes attractions susceptible to the vagaries of weather, which alter visitor numbers and ability to effectively manage revenue.

Yeoman and Leask (1999) identified heritage based attractions exhibit operational and financial seasonal dependency characteristics that makes the need for stronger revenue management to maximize revenue during peak periods. Swarbrooke (1999) suggested success must not be measured by visitor volume, but through visitor spend. Pricing strategies may target market segments and be used effectively to discriminate against visitors as a technique in visitor management particularly where a heritage attraction has reached its carrying capacity. Research by Prentice, Witt and Hamer (1998) indicates there should be a shift away from viewing visitors purely upon socio-economic profiling and move towards a model of benefit segmentation, as it may be a truer reflection of consumer behaviour and willingness to pay.

# 4   Marketing and ideal markets

It has now been firmly established that tourist products are offered to highly segmented consumer markets either through behavioural (Cohen, 1979; Plog, 1973) or archetypal characteristics (e.g. Holloway and Robinson, 1995). Middleton (1996) suggested that culturally there was uniformity in drawing in basic range of segments to visitor attractions irrespective of destination. These segments are broken down into:

1. local residents living within half an hour's drive;

2. regional residents making day visits and travelling up to 2 hours depending upon motivating power of the site;

3. visitors staying with friends and family within about an hour from the site;

4.  visitors staying in serviced or no-serviced accommodation within about an hour;

5.  group travel;

6.  school and educational visits;

Prentice *et al* (1998) recognised the importance of benefit segmentation rather than follow a too generalized socio-economic analysis and ignored the geographic nature of 'ideal markets' which Middleton indicated were important. Getz (1993) modelled the 'tourist business district' in terms of attractions being mutually surrounded and interact with tourism services (i.e. accommodation and transport) and the central functions of government, retail sector, offices and meetings where the access and movement of people were important.

However, this does not fully explain the 'ideal market'. Attractions display spatial characteristics which cannot be simply analysed through distance decay models (Bull, 1995) or consumer profiles. Distance decay assumes the level of activity decreases with distance measured either in time or absolute measurement.

For spatial interaction to take place, there needs to be 'perfect' complementarity i.e. demand in one place has to be matched with supply in another (Ullman, 1956). By using gravity models, marketers of visitor attractions should consider not only market segmentation processes, but also, consider the attractions 'mass' as a pulling power.

Where an intervening opportunity exists, (i.e. alternative supply) an alternative attraction will only be visited by tourists if there is a criteria match. Empirical evidence suggests marketing managers tend to mismatch the degree of competition with other attractions without analyzing their own customer base to check behavioural characteristics.

In terms of pricing strategies, there may be greater emphasis upon consumer perception in 'value for money' and the tourist values than maximization in revenue opportunities through value added processes. Christaller (1966) modelled location in terms of service hierarchy and matched these to distance and sizes of population to produce theoretical ideal markets. In reality 'ideal markets' or catchment areas will produce not a rigid circle or hexagon on a map, but fluid lines based upon the attractions 'mass' and the efficiency of flows within transport systems.

The key to recent growth in many attractions has been matching product development with demographic and life style changes (Fry, 1997). Numerous attractions use pricing structures to attract the over 55's (Ananth, 1992) particularly with grandchildren.

Changes in service provision has aimed at higher quality and more personalized service, for example, membership schemes, timed tickets or restrictions in access to use retail or hospitality services. Attractions have increasingly recognised the importance of a growing secondary role in providing a meeting place where the emphasis is on hospitality or retail provision rather than a repeat visit to the core area of the attraction whether it is an ecclesiastical site, museum, zoo or a themed site.

# 5   Yield management

As the implementation of Yield Management (YM) nears maturity as a management tool, published research now covers airlines (Larsen, 1988; Smith, Leikuhler and Darrow, 1992; Daudel and Vialle 1994; Belobaba and Wilson, 1997; Ingold and Huyton, 1997), hotels (Orkin, 1988; Donaghy, McMahon and McDowell, 1995, tour operations (Hoseason and Johns, 1998; Laws, 1997), cruise and car rental operations.

These studies range from technology impact and implementation studies to marketing, human resource management, revenue and inventory management. Few studies have been made on built visitor attractions whether they are heritage based or theme parks.

Built visitor attractions industry shares a number of common characteristics with other travel and tourism sectors. Both heritage and purpose built visitor attraction sites have capacity relatively constrained either through the carrying capacity of the site or through other factors, for example, planning permission or car parking facilities. Demand is both seasonal and highly segmented (Cross, 1998; Wanhill, 1998; Yeoman and Leask, 1999). Supply may also be constrained through seasonality or, in the case of heritage visitor attractions, through conservation policies.

Subsequently, the different nature in managing organisations where they straddle the public/ private and charity divide, requires fundamentally different strategies for managing revenue even though they may emulate revenue techniques from the private sector. While public sector organisations have to give greater consideration to social cost, the use of revenue maximization techniques may have impact upon funding through central and local government budgetary control. However, shifts in government funding has placed greater dependence on public sector organisations to re-evaluate revenue management and become more empowered and independent in control, making the implementation of YM techniques even more appropriate in their strategies for revenue management.

Kimes (1989, 1997) identifies five necessary conditions for effective YM. These are:

1. fixed capacity;
2. high fixed costs;

3. low variable cost;

4. time - varied demand;

5. similarity of inventory.

Kimes (1989, 1997) augments these conditions with five "necessary ingredients" for the successfully implementation of YM:

1. market segmentation;

2. historical demand and booking patterns;

3. pricing knowledge;

4. overbooking policy;

5. information systems.

Research by Yeoman and Leask (1999) into heritage visitor attractions in Scotland, indicated that visitor attractions match to a greater or lesser extent the core necessary conditions and ingredients in order to implement revenue maximizing techniques. Unlike the accommodation sector visitor attractions are dedicated more specifically to a particular tourist market (Bull, 1995).

Clearly, this indicates a more customized approach to implementation where careful consideration to the site and local conditions must be made. Cross (1998) suggested where markets are mature, over-supplied and showing signs of congestion, organisations need to re-focus on micro-markets for the benefits of effective revenue management to take place and it is here that visitor attractions now need to concentrate.

Schwartz (1998) suggests that the perishability of the product and the customer's willingness to pay are in fact the key elements in YM. The necessary conditions and ingredients identified by Kimes and Cross are often overstated and may be contributing factors and embody misconceptions and misunderstandings of price demand elasticity and consumer behaviour.

Substantial research by numerous authors (notably Lieberman, 1993; Farrell and Whelan-Ryan, 1998; Edgar, 1998) indicates that different sectors of the travel and tourism industry apply YM techniques differently (Smith et al, 1992). Both Orkin (1988) and Lieberman (1993) recognised YM can be effectively implemented without sophisticated computer or management systems.

The Millennium Commission has reported a £4 billion-programme covering over 180 capital projects to celebrate the millennium. In the visitor attractions market, impact studies tended to focus on individual projects at the time of funding bids being made rather than a more holistic approach.

While these projects have upgraded and enabled greater diversity in choice, this type of product development may impact upon pricing strategies (Middleton,

1996; Edgar, 1997; Poon, 1993) in order for new sites to reach critical mass in visitor numbers. Established visitor attractions may have to alter pricing strategies to counter any destabilization and lowering of yield.

Capacity management should therefore be given far higher visibility and inclusion in revenue management processes than Schwartz (1998) credits.

# 6  Data gathering

The methodology incorporated extensive literature searches within the field of YM. As the implementation and research into YM matures the experience and widening of studies enables researchers to draw upon a more extensive pool of knowledge for evaluation.

The research methodology for this investigation reviewed major annual surveys by the English Tourism Council (ETC) and the East of England Tourist Board (EETB) together with other trade publications in order to obtain contemporary information.

In order to obtain empirical data, a semi-structured interview took place with Anne Bloomfield, manager of the EcoTech Centre in order to obtain qualitative data. Questions were designed to reveal not only historic experience of visitor and revenue management, but also to evaluate future development plans in relation to site capacity and segmentation processes.

In addition, responses were being evaluated in relation to the results of two surveys that had recently been undertaken. One survey had been carried out on behalf of the EcoTech Centre and the other on behalf of the members of the Norfolk Tourist Attractions Association (NTAA). Generally, the questionnaires were designed to look at visitor perceptions of the attractions and included standard questions to establish visitor profiles.

The semi-structured interview was designed to cover questions based upon Cross's (1997) core concepts of revenue management in order to establish the EcoTech's management experiences or strategies towards:

- pricing strategies;
- main market segments;
- trends in micro-markets;
- incentives for repeat business;
- establish data on individual organisational experiences in YM;
- booking lead-time trends.

Both questionnaires had been carried out over May to June 2000. The EcoTech Centre included on-site sampling where the focus was on usage and perceptions of facilities on site as well as off-site surveys in adjacent market towns that focussed on awareness. The NTAA survey was intended to establish reasons behind poor attendance by local visitors and to analyze spatial trends within the region by using a number of market towns spread out over the region, but always located near a major attraction.

# 7 Results and discussion

The EETB estimated there were 3.2 million trips to Norfolk where visitors spent £434 million on tourism related services of which 7% were overseas visitors who spent £97 million. In 1998 Norfolk had around 567,000 visits spread across 69 major visitor attractions (EETB, 2000). Since 1995, many attractions within the region have either remained stable or seen a reduction of between 3% and 7.5%. These figures broadly follow known national trends (Hanna, 1999; Howell, 2000). Difficulties in analysis stems from lack in consistency of reported data with a number of attractions not disclosing visitor numbers. The largest attraction, The Pleasure Beach at Great Yarmouth has seen a decline of 30% (600,000 visitors) since 1995 and this reflects the general decline of the resort and a number of poor seasons where weather and international events like Euro '98 impacted upon visits.

A key factor in the performance of any new attractions is being ready for the main tourism season. Although the EcoTech Centre opened in the spring of 1999, delays to building and site completion coupled to poor weather did not turn the opening into a recipe for a disaster, but did impact upon visitor targets. The EcoTech Centre opened to a fanfare of high media coverage and the management team recorded visitor responses from the first day of opening.

Pricing strategies were set well within the range of local attractions and were thought to be 'about right'. Quite early, qualitative research indicated that the first wave of visitors were environmentalists or organisations associated with environmental issues who would turn out to be quite critical of the centre. These groups had a high socio-economic profile of A, B, C1/2 who found the centrepiece exhibition 'Doomsday' re-iterating environmental issues as a core theme, but not offering solutions.

The interpretation boards would not be fully in place until July 1999 that meant the full impact of exhibition material could not be appreciated. Responses clearly indicated to the management team that a successful high profile media campaign was now perceived as media hype. Initial research indicated 40% of the visitors came from Norwich and Kings Lynn that tied in with major newspaper coverage for the region. Even a poor range in stock for the shop received comment. It was anticipated that a major revenue centre would have a poor performance even though gross profit margins are typically between 40 – 60%. There was a reluctance to commit £20,000 towards stock too early in the 'proving' stages.

Operationally, the centre suffered from similar tourist behaviour patterns experienced by other attractions within the area. Themed attractions and heritage properties see falls in attendance when hot weather conditions existed and compete head-on with the beach or zoos. The EcoTech Centre was perceived to be an indoor attraction best suited to colder weather which has brought to the front the need for continued site development to counteract this factor. The centre's design incorporated a passive solar collection system. On hot days visitors and staff found the experimental building too efficient in heat retention and this has caused modification work to be carried out to improve temperature.

With Ecotricity's agreement to build a wind-turbine with a viewing platform, it provided the EcoTech Centre with an additional showcase exhibit and provided a much-needed value-added element to the visit. Due for completion in May 1999, delays in construction and granting of Health & Safety Executive approval forced re-evaluation of visitor targets and the management of revenue as the turbine finally opened during the month of August.

Between April and October 28,500 visitors were attracted to EcoTech, a reduction of 36% from estimates made in the feasibility study. Despite delays and coping with a 'learning curve', the number of visitors was comparable to other visitor centres within Norfolk.

For 2000, pricing strategies (see Appendix 1) were altered and the principles of revenue management (Cross, 1997) were applied even though they were not directly recognised as such. The wind turbine was priced separately with main entrance prices significantly reduced in order to focus on revenue generation from family or single adults with children. Research indicated the over 55's with grandchildren too formed a significant segment of visitors. Their usage of the site would differ from other visitors and the pricing strategy ensured this group's were being met. With a full programme of activities and exhibitions planned for the year, the wind-turbine now provided the USP.

New marketing and pricing strategies could now provide a more dynamic management plan with the shift in focus to micro market segments. With a broadened base, the attraction could now effectively use pricing strategies based upon clear segmentation processes to allow sufficient price discrimination to improve revenue.

A bold decision was made to close the centre on Saturdays during the off-peak period. Market day in Swaffham and 'change-over day' for the regions holiday homes and boats on the Norfolk Broads produced very low visitor numbers. In conjunction with new pricing strategies, a more defined marketing strategy towards a more formalized programme of educational visits for staff and school children was put together with a target of 6,000 visitors.

The impact of the new strategy saw a significant shift in relationships within revenue centres. Figure 2 shows there is a clear indication that the new pricing strategy saw a significant improvement to secondary spend which almost doubled the on-site spend. By implementing micro marketing and pricing strategies, the enhanced on-site spend will begin to compensate for lower visitor numbers through improvement in visitor spend and value.

Consideration must be given to a number of constraints that impact upon the EcoTech Centre and similar attractions in Norfolk. Empirical evidence suggests a number of factors need to be included within the revenue management system. These being:

1. Timing/ planning visits.

2. The size of the ideal market and its capacity.

3. Seasonality.

Day-trippers do not pre-plan trips in the same way as other tourists use cognitive decision making models (Chen, 1997). The research from different locations indicated that between 20-30% decided to visit an attraction on the 'spur of the moment' and between 16% and 35% on the day of visit. Between 15% and 21% would make a decision two days prior to the visit and between 8% and 25% would plan a visit up to a week before.

Less than 23% would make any trip plans more than a week ahead. While weather is a significant element in the planning process, responses across all segments indicated the decision making process was subject to an emotional response within the decision group. No amount of advertising or promotions can fully exploit variance and change influences within these groups.

The second constraint is the concept of the 'ideal market' and threshold population sizes needed to support services (Christaller, 1966). Norfolk has a population of 772,000 and a density of 144 people per sq. Km where 80% of land use is agriculture. In economic location modelling there is insufficient local population to support any of the major attractions within the county and therefore relies heavily upon the 3.2 million visitors to compensate and enable attractions reach threshold figures. While many major Lottery projects have been located within major urban areas within the UK, any expansion in capacity or shortfall in visitor numbers leaves all attractions exposed. Clearly, the future development plans for the EcoTech Centre will broaden its base as an attraction, but as the capacity increases within the visitor attractions market, the exposure to lower performance or constrained opportunity for revenue management, still remains. Empirical evidence also indicates, visitor attractions may be an anomaly within gravity models (Ullman, 1956). Gravity modelling assumes larger the function of place or level in service, human behaviour would follow Newtonian Laws.

Research indicates that local residents under 15 miles from an attraction may not visit an attraction due to a combination of experiential or poor perception of the attraction or by what constitutes a 'day out'. Between 20% and 42% had not visited an attraction adjacent to where they resided and yet between 50% - 70% would travel over 20 miles to an attraction. Fewer than 15% would travel less than 15 miles to an attraction and this creates a 'doughnut' effect around an attraction. Clearly, visitors do not see a local attraction as a 'day out' and this has major implications in marketing and in revenue management. To regain local resident/ visitor confidence in the attraction, highly targeted marketing campaigns with additional concessions will be needed to improve revenue performance from this segment. Capacity management has been identified by Kimes (1989, 1998) and Cross (1997, 1998) as an essential element in YM to be effective. Should there be capacity increases within the region's visitor attractions, then revenue must be expected to fall, unless the volume of visitors into the region has increased, as thresholds may not have been reached.

The third constraint is seasonality (Cross, 1998; Wanhill, 1998; Yeoman and Leask, 1999). EETB figures show 34% of visitors to Norfolk arrive in the period July to September. An additional 26% visit between April to June. However, the statistics do not show the peak in activity spans only a 6 - 8 week period across July and August where operational efficiency is at its peak. Yeoman and Leask (1999) suggested seasonality increased the need for revenue maximizing techniques to be implemented to offset low season performance. For the EcoTech Centre, educational visits and specialist activities, particularly during half term and holidays must be given higher profile than in the past if revenue enhanced techniques are to be used to improve overall performance.

# 8   Conclusions

Yield management is designed to optimise revenue. Institutional change and the greater need for more effective revenue management may govern pressure upon all organisations to improve revenue performance. The EcoTech Centre is severely constrained by the economic thresholds that operate within the ideal market locally. There is insufficient population to support the regions' attractions without the seasonal influx of 3.2 million visitors. The 'doughnut effect' which surrounds the attractions has major implications towards revenue management. Marketing and revenue management strategies need to re-focus their attention on this segment as local residents within 15 miles of an attraction form the threshold for survival. Add an element of seasonality together with performance in weather and all of the attractions then become very exposed to marginalized revenue performance. Too little attention has been paid at national and regional level in terms of the changes in capacity through Lottery funded projects. One of the greatest impacts upon Norfolk attractions in 2001 will be the re-opening of a high-tech interactive display at the Castle Museum, Norwich. Competition amongst the educational sector will be particularly sharp. As the EcoTech Centre matures as a visitor attraction, the plans to build an experimental house together with the interactive walk-through-composting exhibit will become critical to the long-term success of the centre. The behaviour of the micro-market segments is the essence of successful revenue management implementation. Without a continued programme of innovative exhibitions and site development, the EcoTech Centre will fail one of its original objectives i.e. experimentation and innovation.

Figure 1: Correlation between number visitors and shop revenue

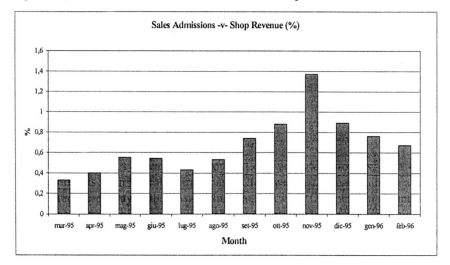

Source: East of England Tourist Board (2000)

# Appendix

EcoTech Discovery Admission Prices 2000. (Centre only). Source: The EcoTech Centre

| Category | £ | % Change |
|---|---|---|
| **Adults** | 4.00 | -20 |
| **Children** (up to 15yrs) | 3.25 | -7.14 |
| **Concessions** (Senior citizens etc) | 3.50 | -17.6 |
| **Family Tickets** | | |
| 2 Adults + 2 Children | 11.00 | N/A |
| 2 Adults + 3 Children | 11.00 | N/A |
| 2 Adults + 1 Child | 9.00 | N/A |
| 1 Adult + 2 Children | 9.00 | N/A |
| 1Adult + 3 Children | 9.00 | N/A |
| **Grandparents** | | |
| 2 Grandparents + 2 Children | 8.00 | N/A |
| 2 Grandparents + 3 Children | 8.00 | N/A |

**Note:** Access to Wind Turbine an additional £1.90 per adult and £1.30 per child

# References

Ananth M. De Micco F. & Howey R., *Marketplace lodging needs of mature travellers*, Cornell Hotel and Restaurant Administration Quarterly, 33, No. 4, 12 – 24, 1992.

Anon, *Marking the close of the second millennium and celebrating the start of the third millennium*, The annual accounts of the Millennium Commission, 1998 –1999, The Stationary Office, UK, 2000

Belobaba P.P & Wilson J.L., *Impacts of yield management in competitive airline markets*, Journal of Air Transport Management, Vol. 3, No. 1 pp. 3 – 10, 1997.

Bull A., *The Economics of Travel and Tourism*, 2nd edn; Longman UK, 1995

Chen J., *The Tourists' Cognitive Decision Making Model*, The Tourist review, No. 4, pp. 4-9, 1997

Christaller W., *Central Places in Southern Germany*, translated C.W Baskin, Englewood Cliffs, Prentice-Hall, USA, 1966

Cohen E., *A Phenomenology of Tourist Experiences*, Sociology, Vol. 13, 1979, pp. 179 – 2001

Cross R.G., *Launching the Rocket, How Revenue management Can Work for Your Business*, Cornell Hotel and Restaurant Administration Quarterly, April, 1997, pp 32 – 43.

Cross R.G., *Revenue Management*, Orion Business Books, UK, 1998

Crouch D.I., *Encounters with leisure / tourism*, in Crouch, D.I (ed) Leisure / Tourism Geographies: practices and geographic knowledge, Routledge, UK, 1999

Daudel S & Vialle G., *Yield Management: Applications to air transport and other service industries*, Institut du Transport Aerien, Paris, 1994.

Dickinson R & Vladimir A., *Selling the Sea - An Inside Look at the Cruise Industry*, John Wiley and Sons, USA/ Canada, 1997

D' Hauteserre A.M., *Disneyland Paris: A Permanent Growth Pole in the Francilian Landscape*, Progress in Tourism and Hospitality Research, Vol. 3, 1997, pp. 17 – 33.

Donaghy K & McMahon U., *Managing yield: a marketing perspective*, Journal of Vacation Marketing, Vol. 2,1, 1995, pp. 55-62.

Donaghy K; McMahon U & McDowell D., *Managing yield: an overview*, International Journal Hospitality Management, Vol. 14, 2, 1995, pp. 139 - 150.

Donaghy K; McMahon-Beattie U & McDowell D., *Implementing yield management: lessons from the hotel sector*, International Journal of Contemporary Hospitality Management, Vol. 9, No. 2, 1995, pp. 50 – 54.

East of England Tourist Board, *Facts of Tourism 1998*, EETB, Hadleigh, 2000.

Edgar D.A., *Economic aspects*, in Yeoman, I & Ingold A (Editors.), Yield Management: Strategies for the Service Industry, Cassell, UK, 1997, pp. 12 – 28.

Edgar D.A., *Yielding: Giants vs. minnows, is there a difference ?*, Progress in Tourism and Hospitality Research, Vol. 4, No. 3, 1998, pp. 255-265.

Farrell K. & Whelan-Ryan F., *Yield Management - A Model for Implementation*, Progress in Tourism and Hospitality Research, Vol. 4, No. 3, 1998, pp. 267-277.

Fry A., *Shades of grey*, Marketing, April 24th, 1997, pp. 23 – 24.

Getz D., *Planning for Tourism Business Districts*, Annals of Tourism Research: Vol. 20, 1993, pp. 583 – 600.

Hall C.M. & Page S.J., The Geography of Tourism and recreation, environment, Place and space, Routledge, UK, 1999

Hanna M., *Visitor Trends at Attractions*, Insights, ETC, London, 1999

Higgins B., *From Growth Poles to Systems of Interactions in Space*, Journal of Growth and Change, Vol. 14, No. 4, 1983, pp. 3 - 13.

Holloway J.C., *The Business of Tourism*, 5th edn, Addison Wesley Longman, UK, 1998

Hoseason J.M. & Johns N., *The Numbers Game: The role of yield management in the tour operations industry*, Progress in Tourism and Hospitality Research, Vol. 4, No. 3, 1998, pp. 197 – 206.

Howell D., *The role of leisure and theme parks in the new Millennium*, Insights, ETC, London, 2000

Ingold A. & Huyton J.R., *Yield management in the Airline Industry*, in Yeoman, I & Ingold A (Editors.), Yield Management: Strategies for the Service Industry, Cassell, UK, 1997, pp. 143 – 159.

Kimes S., *The basics of Yield Management*, The Cornell HRA Quarterly, Vol.3, No. 3 November, 1989, pp. 14 – 19.

Kimes S., *Yield management: An overview*, in Yeoman, I and Ingold, A (Editors.), Yield Management: Strategies for the Service Industry, Cassell, UK, 1997, pp 3 – 11.

Larsen T.D., *Yield management and your passengers*, ASTA Agency Magazine, June, 1988, pp. 46 – 48.

Laws E., *Perspectives on Pricing Decisions in the Inclusive Holiday Industry*, in Yeoman, I and Ingold, A (Editors.), Yield Management : Strategies for the Service Industry, Cassell, UK, 1997, pp. 67 – 82.

Lieberman W.H., *Debunking the Myths of YM*, The Cornell HRA Quarterly, Vol. 34, No. 1, 1993, pp. 34 – 41.

McClarence S., *Look on my works, ye mighty..?*, Times Weekend, April 20th, 2000.

Middleton V.T.C., *Marketing in Travel and Tourism*, 2nd edn, Heinemann, UK, 1996

Orkin E.B., *Yield Management makes forecasting fact not fiction*, Hotel and Motel Management, August 15, 1988, pp. 112 - 118.

Plog S.C., *Why Destinations Rise and Fall in Popularity*, Los Angeles: Unpublished manuscript of the Travel Research Association, 1973. This has subsequently appeared in the public domain as: Plog, S. C., *Why Destination Areas Rise and Fall in Popularity* in Domestic and International Tourism, edited by E. M. Kelly, Wellesley Mass: Institute of Certified Travel Agents, 1977

Poon A., *Tourism, Technology and Competitive Strategies,* CAB International Press, Wallingford, 1993.

Prentice R.C., Witt S.F. & Hamer C., *Tourismas Experience: The Case of Heritage Parks,* Annals of Tourism Research, Vol. 25, No. 1, 1998, pp. 1 – 24.

Schwartz Z., *The confusing side of yield management: myths, errors and misconceptions,* Journal of Hospitality and Tourism Research, No. 4, 1998, pp. 413 – 430.

Sinden J.A. & Worrell A.C., *Unpriced values,* Wiley, New York, 1979.

Smith B.C., Leimkuhler J.F. & Darrow R.M., *Yield management at American Airlines,* Interfaces, Vol. 22 No. 1, 1992, pp. 8 – 31.

Swarbrooke J., The development and Management of Visitor Attractions, Butterworth-Heinemann, Oxford, 1999.

Ullman E., *The Role of Transport and the Bases for Interaction*, in W.L Thomas (ed) Man's Role in Changing the face of the Earth, University of Chicago Press, USA, 1956

Wanhill S., *Attractions,* in Cooper, C et al (eds) Tourism: Principles and Practice, 2nd Edn, Longman, UK, 1998

# Revenue management in the restaurant sector

## Charlotte R. Rassing

Institut for Konjunktur Analyse
Aaberaa 29
1124 Copenhagen
Denmark

*Contents: 1 Background information. 1.1 Purpose and composition of the paper. 2 Introduction. 3 Literature review. 4 Implications for the use of revenue management. 5 Complexity of pricing in the restaurant sector. 6 Menu analysis. 7 Empirical study to be undertaken. References. Appendix. Questionnaire.*

# 1 Background information

The beginning of 2000 a new tourism research centre in Denmark was founded Centre without walls (Center uden mure} The centre is a consortium of Roskilde University, Copenhagen, Business School (institute for management, politics and philosophy) and the Research Centre of Bornholm. The research program that has to take place during the next three years is partly founded by the Danish Social Science Research Council. As part of this program a Ph.D. study at the Research Centre of Bornholm has been offered under the title Revenue Management in the Restaurant Sector. The Ph.D. student will be registered in Bournemouth University, UK, but the daily work will take place at the Research centre of Bornholm, Denmark.

The objectives of the Ph.D. project is (1) to extend the theory of revenue management into the area of food and beverage operations, so as to product new processes in pricing, menu analysis and budgeting, and (2) to work with HORESTA (the Danish Hotels, Restaurant and Tourist Businesses Association) and selected restaurants in Bornholm to develop applications which have immediate practical returns to the sector.

## 1.1 Purpose and composition of the paper

The purpose of this paper is to introduce the reader to the Ph. D research that has to be undertaken at the Research centre of Bornholm within the next three years.

The first part of the paper will take a closer look at what literature already exists about revenue management and what has to be done to apply the theory to the restaurant sector. In the second part of the paper the empirical research to be undertaken will be briefly presented both the ideas and the expected output. It is important to point out that the Ph. D project is still at its very beginning. Therefore most of this paper will deal with already existing research and ideas to research in the future.

# 2 Introduction

Within the food and beverages industry revenue management is defined by Farell, K. and Whelan-lyan, F. (1998) as "the allocation of fixed capacity to various segmented markets in such a way as to meet customer requirements and to provide maximum returns on available capacity by the application of discriminatory pricing".

Revenue management includes all kinds of price discrimination that can be used to maximise the revenue when the capacity is fixed (HOREST A, 1999} The theory was developed, coined for and refined by the airline industry following airline deregulation in the 1970s. Today the technique is widely accepted and extensively used throughout the world, mainly among large hotels (Baum, T and Mudambi, R., 1998, p. 68) but also among large cruise liners, tour operators, and car rental companies. As far as the author knows, and according to experts within the field of revenue management, the theory has not yet been applied to the restaurant sector.

Some authors (Kimes, S.E., et al, 1998; Kimes, S.E., 1999) are occupied with the theoretical aspects of revenue management in relation to the restaurant sector, however as van Westering, J. stated in 1994 (p 140) still seems to be true "the theory is far in advance of the practical application of YM".

The research into food and beverages has tended to tackle singular problems rather than taking a holistic review (van Westering, J., 1994} Historically there has been much focus on optimising the average meal rate or the number of visitors in the restaurant. When the focus is on the number of customers this tends to encourage the sale of discounted meals (two courses for the price of one, two meals for the price of the most expensive, etc.).

Even though this could be a profitable strategy it sets focus on volume rather than value. To focus on the average check also leaves out important information. High paying customers could be lingering over their meal and occupying the table for a long period of time leaving other customers waiting. The objective of revenue management in the restaurant sector is to go beyond traditional thinking and make a composite measure of average meal rate and number of visitors. The idea is to shift from product-orientation to demand-orientation

# 3   Literature review

Revenue management, also called yield management, capacity management, revenue enhancement or perishable asset revenue management, is said to be (Donaghy, K., 1996) "the most important working tool available to the lodging and hospitality industry for business planning".

In literature revenue management is described as the process of allocating the right capacity to the right customer at the right time in order to maximise revenue or yield (Smith, BC. et al, 1992; Hanks, R.D. et al, 1992; Donaghy, K., 1996; Kimes, S.E., 1997; Donaghy, K. et al, 1998; Kimes, S.E. et al, 1998; Farrell, K. and Whelan-Ryan, F., 1998; Yeoman, L. and Watson, S., 1997; Orkin, E.B., 1998)

The idea is to maximise an enterprise's effective use of its resources by moving away from mass pricing and mass marketing, to the management of the micro market. It is an approach to increasing revenues and improving customer service by responding to current and expected demand (Lieberman, W.H., 2000) and is based on three factors. people, forecasting and strategy (Yeoman, L and Watson, S, 1997).

Revenue management is build on facts about the past, what is known about the present and current trends and what is likely to happen in the future i.e. projected levels of business (Donaghy, K. et al, 1995; Donaghy, K. 1996)

The key to the application of revenue management theories is the predictability in the behaviour of specific market segments within overall market demand. The restaurant sector is faced with a variety of customer segments with quite different demands (Hiemstra, S.J., 1998)

These demands vary according to the purpose of the visit to the restaurant (basic need for eating, pleasure, celebration, business etc.) The capability of continually monitoring and forecasting changes in these demand patterns is crucial to the successful implementation of revenue management. Revenue management activities must be based on a comprehensive awareness of continually changing market configurations (Donaghy, K. and McMahon, U, 1995) and it requires knowledge of customers' expected behaviour, plus an understanding of which business is most beneficial/profitable (Quain, W.J. et al, 1999).

As stated by Muller, C.C. (1999) the restaurateurs have to be aware of both predictable, seasonal factors and unpredictable, individual customer demand - a combination of macro-predictability and micro-uncertainty. A systematic approach and combination of knowledge, experience, understanding and forecasting will help the restaurant to succeed in a very fast changing environment.

# 4 Implications for the use of revenue management

Revenue management is seen as applicable and of interest to businesses where the following conditions prevail (Kimes, S.E. et al, 1998; Smith, B.C. et al, 1992; Brotherton, B. and Mooney, S., 1992; Hanks et al, 1992; Donaghy, K. and McMahon, U., 1995; European Commission, 1997; Cross, R.G., 1997; Yeoman, I. and Ingold, A., 1997; Vogel, H. et al, 1998).

1.  Where capacity is relatively fixed.

2.  When demand can be separated into distinct market segments/offer a range of customer values (different prices available).

3.  When stock inventory is perishable so that timing of sale is important.

4.  When the product is sold well in advance of consumption/allow advance reservations.

5.  Where cancellations and no-shows are experienced.

6.  When demand fluctuates substantially/seasonal and other demand peaks.

7.  Where marginal sales costs of selling an additional unit are low and fixed costs are high.

8.  Where rapidly changing market circumstances exist.

9.  Where there is an ability to forecast future demands.

10. Where there is an ability to segment customers on their varying needs, behaviour, and willingness to pay.

The restaurant sector can nod their acquaintance to the conditions but obviously needs to concretise, adjust and specify them according to the restaurant sector's specific needs. It seems very important to clarify the differences between the sectors where revenue management has already been applied (airlines and hotels) and the restaurant sector. The root concepts are the same, but the applications and the techniques used to implement the concepts will vary widely. Airlines and hotels have been working with revenue management for years. Even though especially hotels and restaurants have many similarities (i.e. different arrival times during the day and relatively fixed capacity) there are also important differences that need to be highlighted.

Both hotels and restaurants use day of the week to differentiate prices. Furthermore hotels use length of stay (among other factors) to differentiate price while restaurants use time of the day (among other factors). Restaurants operate with smaller time periods and considerably more variables than hotels and airlines (Muller, C.C. 1999). A menu can easily be composed of more than 100 items, each of which need to be separately costed, prepared, served and accounted for on the customer's bill (National Restaurant Association, 1990) A restaurant can meet many small transactions during one day and has many employees who handle cash. In both hotels and restaurants the demand pattern consists of customers who make reservations and customers who walk in. However, the distribution between the two groups of customers is very different. Restaurants typically experience a smaller proportion of advance reservations than hotels.

In restaurants opposite hotels some regular periods of the day will obviously be busier than others. Especially during lunch and dinnertime there can be pressure on the capacity measured by seating, kitchen capacity, menu items, and/or staff (Kimes, S.E. et al, 1998).

When a customer enters a restaurant the tangible product is the meal but the customer also buys an experience consisting of many components: reception, table assignment, table location, ordering acceptance, food delivery etc. - a complex mixture of service, atmosphere and mood. All this makes pricing for restaurants very complex.

The hotel room is a perishable product and a parallel can be drawn to a seat in a restaurant. A seat that goes unfilled is gone forever but it is not as simple as that. The food can be stored for some period of time and directing the customers' attention towards specific menus can reduce losses.

Revenue management primary focus is often regarded as maximisation of sales revenue but can be seen as a concept of further extension in terms of the development of an optimum business mix to maintain profitable product-market alignment (Edgar, D.A., 1997). The goal of implementing revenue management in the restaurant sector is to maximise revenue per available seat-hour (Rev P. ASH) by manipulating price and meal duration (Kimes, SE. 1999) It has been defined as selling the right seat to the right customer at the right price and for the right duration

# 5 Complexity of pricing in the restaurant sector

In 'Pricing and yield management' (1998, p. 4) it is pointed out that "improvements in price typically have three to four times the effect that proportional increases in sales volume have on profit levels". Therefore success in the food service area is dependent on the development of the right menu-pricing system (Miller, J .E., 1992, p. 104 } The price of the items on the menu will ultimately determine the success or failure of the restaurant. Both economic and strategic objectives have to be taken into consideration when the restaurant decides on its pricing policy. A higher menu price seems more acceptable to the customers if it is followed by additional service. Simply put, value to a restaurant's guests is enhanced by an increase in the quality of food, service, decor etc., or by a decrease in the tariff associated with the dining experience (Orkin, E.B., 1978) It is important to keep in mind that each restaurant is unique when it comes to pricing. Depending of the history of the restaurant as well as the number of years in business and the supplier arrangements, the restaurants can have very different expenses to start off with. The costs of providing a product or service must be incorporated into the price charged. When it comes to pricing different items on a menu qualitative aspects also have to be taken into consideration. At the end of the day the restaurateur has to be able to offer a product with an acceptable gross profit margin at an acceptable price for the customer

The restaurant's price level tells the consumers something about the product offered: the quality. By manipulating price in combination with product quality and promotional messages, the product can be differentiated or standardised (Pricing and yield management, 1998, p. 3) A price is a complex phenomenon The price has to reflect both the food costs (cost of raw material) and preparation At the same time it can reflect the atmosphere, different kinds of entertainment, specific service, product presentation etc. If the customers feel they achieve an additional value they will be willing to pay more. If the product cannot satisfy the consumers' needs and expectations, the customers are not going to return. The essential part of pricing is meeting the restaurant's need for profit making and combine that need with customers' need for value for money. Customer attitudes will dictate what is acceptable (Miller, JE., 1992, p. 105}

To succeed in adapting the concepts of revenue management the individual restaurant must have a clear understanding of the menu sales mix and the contribution margin of each menu item. Costs include all overhead, labour, food, and beverage cost The highest contribution margin may not come from the highest-priced menu items (the valuable customer is not always the profitable customer) and the waiters need to know where to focus the attention of today's customers in the ordering process. The place to focus may very well change during the day and the week. The essence of revenue management is not new to the restaurant sector. Many businesses are using sub-components from the theory: offering a specific lunch menu that costs less than the same menu in the evening, charging different prices on weekdays compared with weekends ( depending on the target group} offering specific menus if the customers order in advance in connection with their booking - menus that are not available otherwise, etc. What is new to the restaurants is the systematic approach towards pricing and menu planning that the adoption of revenue management will result in.

# 6 Menu analysis

Revenue management focuses the management decision-process on the maximisation of profits from sale of the core product: the menu item. The main product in a restaurant is seen to be food and the menu is thus the principal means of selling (Cattet, A. and Smith, C., 1994). The customers have to rely totally on the menu for all communications about the products, as they cannot examine the products beforehand. The choice of menu item (the intangible item) has to be based on the tangible clues that surround it. Customers can reduce the risk of miss-purchase by examining the clues given on the restaurant's food and the services before entering the place. If the menu is well made it will lead customers to buy the items with the highest gross profit margin - the dishes the restaurant wishes to sell.

The social and demographic profile of a restaurant's customers must have a major impact on the menu. Different food products, cooking styles and ingredients are continuing to appear and influence the menu content and have to be directed towards the target group of customers. The menu is the ultimate profit centre of the restaurant and must always be the focal point. How well the customer can see, read and understand the menu item description will affect how well the dish will sell. Restaurants have to structure their menu formats around the needs of their customers as well as the limitations of the kitchen (Cattet, A and Smith, C., 1994). The menu functions as the communication tool between the restaurateur and the customers.

# 7   Empirical study to be undertaken

The main intention of revenue management is to shift from cost oriented pricing towards market oriented pricing. During the summer 2000 a questionnaire and letter of introduction will be designed and mailed to HORESTA for their comments (temporary draft for the questionnaire is enclosed as appendix 1) In the late summer a pilot survey will be carried out among 10-20 restaurants and the questionnaire will be corrected according to the responses. During the autumn of 2000 the questionnaire will be mailed to all 900 restaurants (except the participants in the pilot survey) in Denmark who are members of HORESTA. The idea is, though this quantitative study, to throw light on the typical pricing procedures used among restaurants in Denmark and thereby find out what aspects are taken into consideration when different items on a menu arc priced. The survey will provide an indication to what degree the restaurants in Denmark are still focused on traditional cost pricing or moving towards market oriented pricing, that is. to what extent the restaurants are using elements of revenue management in their daily pricing procedures and menu planning. The research undertaken will mainly apply to services restaurants. Fast-food establishments and industry kitchens do not share the same kind of problems.

As can be seen from appendix I, the restaurants will be asked if they wish to take part in a further co-operation. About 20 of the restaurants, which agree to participate, will be used as case studies in the further research. If more than 20 agree to participate, a selection process has to take place. This process has not yet been decided but the idea is to choose different types of service restaurants. Thereby the results can be widened and made usable and useful to more restaurants. Both quantitative numbers (accounts) and qualitative statements (personal interviews) will be used to go further into the procedure of pricing and menu planning in the restaurants.

In mathematical modelling terms, the iterative process of pricing and budgeting, is one of solving a set of simultaneous equations subject to certain constraints, both qualitative, in terms of providing a cuisine that is consistent with the meal experience that is being offered, and quantitative, in terms of the pattern and volume of demand. It should be possible to model these processes so as to provide a mathematical tool to assist in setting menu prices and sales volumes that are consistent with overall food and beverage budget targets. Such a tool will be developed as software and made available to restaurant operations. The data from the restaurants will be used in the construction phase and testing of the model.

# References

Baum T. & Mudambi R., *Empirical analysis of oligopolistic hotel pricing*, in Economic and Management Methods for Tourism and Hospitality Research, ed Baum, T. and Mudambi, R., Wiley, England, 1998, p. 68.

Brotherton B. & Mooney S., *Yield Management - progress and prospects*, International Journal of Hospitality Management, Vol. I, No. 1, 1992, pp. 23 - 32.

Cattet A. & Smith C., *The menu as a marketing tool*, in Progresses in Tourism, Recreation and Hospitality Management, ed. Cooper C. P. and Lockwood A, Wiley, Chichester, ch. 12, 1994, pp. 149 - 163.

Cross R.G., *Launching the Revenue Rocket. How Revenue Management Can Work for Your Business*, Cornell Hotel and Restaurant Administration Quarterly, Vol. 38, No. 2, 1997, pp. 32 - 43.

Donaghy K., *Plotting future profits with yield management*, Hospitality, February/March, 1996, pp. 18 - 19.

Donaghy K. & McMahon U., *Managing yield: a marketing perspective*, Journal of Vacation Marketing, Vol. 2, No I, 1995, pp. 55 - 62.

Donaghy K., McMahon U & McDowell D., *Yield Management an overview*, International Journal of Contemporary Hospitality Management, Vol. 14, No. 2, 1995, pp. 139 - 150.

Donaghy K., McMahon-Beattie U., Yeoman I. & Ingold A., *The Realism of Yield Management*, Progress in Tourism and Hospitality Research, Vol. 4, No. 3, 1998, pp. 187 - 196.

Edgar D.A., *Economic Aspects*, in Yield Management Strategies for the Service Industries, ed. Yeoman, I. and Ingold, A., Cassell, London, 1997, pp. 12 - 28.

European Commission, *Yield Management in small and medium-sized enterprises in the tourism industry*, Executive summary, Directorate-General XXII, 1997.

Farrell K. & Whelan-Ryan F., *Yield Management - a Model for Implementing*, Progress in Tourism and Hospitality Research, Vol. 4, No. 3, 1998, pp. 267 - 277.

Hanks R.D., Cross R.G. & Noland R.P., *Discounting in the Hotel Industry. A New Approach*, Cornell Hotel and Restaurant Administration Quarterly, Vol. 33, No. 1, 1992, pp. 15 - 23.

Hiemstra S.J., *Economic Pricing Strategies for Hotels*, in Economic and Management Methods for Tourism and Hospitality Research, ed. Baum, T. and Mudambi, R., Wiley, England, 1998, pp. 215 - 231.

Horesta, *Notes from Yield Management course*, 19th-20th of April and 3rd-4th May 1999, in Danish, 1999

Kimes S.E., *Yield Management: An Overview*, in Yield Management Strategies for the Service Industries, ed. by Coman, I. and Ingold, A., Cassell, London, 1997, pp. 3 - 11.

Kimes S.E., *Implementing Restaurant Revenue Management a Five-step Approach*, Cornell Hotel and Restaurant Administration Quarterly, Vol. 40, No. 3, 1999, pp. 16 - 21.

Kimes S.E., Chase R.B., Choi S., Lee P.Y. & Ngonzi E.N., *Restaurant Revenue Management Applying Yield Management to the Restaurant Industry*, Cornell Hotel and Restaurant Administration Quarterly, Vol. 39, No.3, 1998, pp. 32 - 39.

Lieben Ian W., *Yield Management System or Program?*, Veritec Solutions, 2000 www.veritecsolutions.com.

Miller J.E., *Menu Pricing & Strategy,* Third edition, Van Nostrand Reinhold, New York, 1992.

Muller C.C., *A Simple Measure of Restaurant Efficiency*, Cornell Hotel and Restaurant Administration Quarterly, Vol. 40, No. 3, 1999, pp. 31 - 37.

National Restaurant Association, *Uniform System of Accounts for Restaurants,* Sixth revised edition, prepared by Laventhol & Horwath, Washington, D.C., 1990

Orkin E.B., *An Integrated Menu-Pricing System*, Cornell Hotel and Restaurant Administration Quarterly, No. 19, 1978, pp. 8 - 13.

Orkin E.B., *Wishful Thinking and Rocket Science. The Essential Matter of Calculating Unconstrained Demand for Revenue Management*, Cornell Hotel and Restaurant Administration Quarterly, Vol. 39, No.4, 1998, pp. 15-19.

*Pricing and yield management*, Marketing for success a practical guide for tourism business, Ireland, 1998.

Quain B., Sansbury M. & Wand Lebruto S.M., *Revenue Enhancement, Part 4 -Increasing Restaurant Profitability*, Cornell Hotel and Restaurant Administration Quarterly, Vol. 40, No. 3, 1999, pp. 38 - 47.

Smith B.C., Leimkuhler J.F. & Darrow R.M., *Yield management at American airlines*, Interface, Vol. 22, No. I, 1992, pp. 8 - 31.

Van Westering, J., *Yield management: the case for food and beverage operations*, in Progress in Tourism, Recreation and Hospitality Management, ed. Cooper C P and Lockwood A, Wiley, Chichester, ch. II, 1994, pp. 139 - 148.

Vogel, Horand and Associates, *AHI Hotel Yield Management Seminar Series Europe '98*, seminar notes, 1998.

Yeoman I. & Watson S., *Yield management a human activity system*, Contemporary Hospitality Management, Vol. 9, No. 2, 1997, pp. 80 - 83.

# Appendix

To the restaurants

[ name and contact person ]

My name is Charlotte Rassing. I am employed as a Ph.D. researcher at the Research Centre of Bornholm. During the next three years I will be working on a project about pricing and menu planning in the restaurant sector. The idea is to establish a program that can assist the restaurants when it comes to pricing and menu planning and thereby help to remarkably increase the earnings of the restaurants.

The theory I am working with is called *Revenue Management*. One of the basic elements in the theory is price differentiation, which is used by most of the restaurants already. Many restaurants offer specific lunch courses at favourable prices, packaged meals (soup-roast-ice cream) at special prices, etc.

The restaurants have for a long period of time been focusing on increasing the number of customers or average rate per meal The intention of *Revenue Management* is to a larger degree to focus on earnings.

My project is still in the first phase. Therefore I need your help to identify the restaurant sectors present pricing methods. In connection to that I very much hope that your are able to spare five minutes to fill in the enclosed questionnaire and possibly give your permission for further co-operation The idea with the further co-operation is to work with your specific restaurant and how your revenue can be increased. The granting will of course be free of charge

All data will be treated with confidentiality.

Thank you very much for your help.

 Yours faithfully

Charlotte Rassing

Please enclose a copy of your menu.

# Questionnaire

When you price an item on your menu, which of the following factors do you take into consideration?

| | Always | Often | Some-times | Rarely | Never | Don't know |
|---|---|---|---|---|---|---|
| A feeling of what the customers are willing to pay | | | | | | |
| Knowledge of competitors' prices | | | | | | |
| The price of the food in the item | | | | | | |
| The direct labour involved in the preparation of the item (chef) | | | | | | |
| The total labour involved in relation to the item (salary to chef, waiter, etc) | | | | | | |
| Consideration of the total desired revenue | | | | | | |
| Consideration of the total profit | | | | | | |
| An average amount the item has to cover of the fixed costs (rent,. salary to restaurateur, interest, etc.) | | | | | | |
| Knowledge of the restaurants total expenses (food costs, salaries, rent, interests, etc) | | | | | | |
| I will set my prices close to competitors' | | | | | | |
| I will set my own prices regardless of the competitors' price level | | | | | | |
| I will set my prices and adjust them according to markets reactions | | | | | | |
| I will try to price below competitors' price level to attract more customers | | | | | | |

# Revenue management and food service businesses: the case of Italy

## Emanuela Schiaffella

e.schiaffella@cstassisi.it.

Italian Centre for Advanced Studies in Tourism and Tourism Promotion (CST)

Via C. Cecci, 1 – 06088 – Assisi (PG) – Italy

*Contents: 1 The food service sector in Italy. 1.1 The food service supply and demand in Italy: a reference summary. 1.1.1 Sector data: the food service supply. 1.1.2 The food service demand. 2 Revenue management and food service businesses. 2.1 Applicability of revenue management. 2.1.1 Overview. 2.1.2 Applicability requirements and food service businesses. 2.2 Revenue management and Italian food service businesses: application difficulties. 2.2.1 Structural limits. 2.2.2 Managerial limitations.*

# 1 The food service sector in Italy

## 1.1 The food service supply and demand in Italy: a reference summary

### 1.1.1 Sector data: the food service supply

In Italy, based on the results of the *Federazione Italiana Pubblici Esercizi*[1], in 2003, 74.749 food service businesses were registered, distributed in this way:

| Location | Absolute value | Percentage |
|---|---|---|
| North West | 19.878 | 26,59% |
| North East | 17.305 | 23,15% |
| Centre | 15.137 | 20,25% |
| South / Islands | 22.429 | 30,01% |
| **Italy** | **74.749** | **100,00%** |

---

[1] Italian Federation of Commercial Businesses. Data drawn from www.fipe.it "The numbers of the sector (2003)"

The supply is extremely pulverised, composed of small independent businesses, often family-run and with a seasonal type of activity, and fragmented into numerous types[2]; confirming the data from 2002 [3], a composition is taking shape of the following Italian food service offer, expressed in percentages:

|                                      | %     |
|--------------------------------------|-------|
| Small restaurants                    | 17,4  |
| Family restaurants                   | 8,3   |
| Pizza restaurants                    | 25,1  |
| Seasonal restaurants                 | 7,2   |
| Large banquet restaurants            | 1,3   |
| Fixed-menu eateries                  | 8,7   |
| Small restaurants with many workers  | 9,8   |
| Large restaurants /pizza restaurants | 1,6   |
| Taverns/pubs/eateries                | 20,6  |
| **Total**                            | **100,0** |

To this type of food service, so-called *commercial*, one must add *industrial* food service, composed of collective, military, scholastic, hospital, religious and community food service, which is characterised , in line with the rest of Europe, by a polarisation among a few large companies and a myriad of minor operators[4].

As has been mentioned before, the Italian food service business is on the average small scale, with about 79 seats in interior spaces and, where available, 50 seats outside [5]. Only 34,5% of all structures have a personal computer; 26,2% of these are connected to Internet and 16,7% use this connection for business purposes[6].

## 1.1.2 The food service demand

As far as the demand is concerned, in the last decade, food consumption outside of

---

[2]   Maria Del Duca, *Integrazione produttiva e specializzazione di mercato: nuove tecnologie e processi interni di lavoro nel comparto ristorativi* (Production integration and market specialisation: new technology and internal work processes for the food service sector), in Stefano Poeta (ed.), *L'analisi dei fabbisogni formativi e professionali del settore turismo* (Analysis of the professional training needs of the tourism industry), FrancoAngeli s.r.l. Milan, Italy, 2000.

[3]   Elaborazioni FIPE, Convention Mixer, Montecarlo 27 September 2002 (www.fipe.it)

[4]   With a world food service value estimated at 1.300 billion euros, the European area is worth about 22%, or 280 billion euros. In the context of the European turnover, the *top ten* companies, with Autogrill, - the only Italian group - ranking tenth, register sales amounting to 33,8 billion euros, that is 12% of organised European food service. Autogrill, the leading Italian company, registered 1,1 billion euros in sales in the European market. It is interesting to observe that, in almost all sectors, the market leader is British (with Compact Group for catering, Scottish and Newcastle for cafeterias, etc.). These observations have been drawn from the trade magazine Ristorazione collettiva, April 2003

[5]   Elaborazioni FIPE, Convention Mixer, Montecarlo 27 September 2002 (www.fipe.it)

[6]   Elaborazioni FIPE, idem

the home, in Italy, has been in continual expansion: in 1992, 25,7% of food spending regarded food consumed outside the home, compared to 31,2% in 2002 [7].

In line with the increase in extra-domestic food consumption, other variations have been found in eating habits, for example [8]:

- the role of the evening meal is growing in an identical way: compared to a de-structured lunch consumed outside the home (both for economic reasons and because of the pace of work), the evening meal becomes the complete meal;
- the classical combination of the Italian meal is changing (first course, second course, vegetable, dessert) with the development of the buffet-style food service offer;
- less elaborate and more digestible foods and cooking methods are preferred;
- there is greater awareness of the reception, the aesthetics, the friendliness of personnel.

In this context, although traditional Italian food service is still prevalent, the current and future trend is that of heading towards new, different and innovative formulas.

# 2 Revenue management and food service businesses

## 2.1 Applicability of revenue management

### 2.1.1 Overview

Revenue management is one of the more innovative phenomena which have characterised the management of tourist businesses in the last fifteen years. Experience has demonstrated that such a system can really contribute to increasing a company's revenue, through management following models that keep in mind the particulars related to the production capacity of the business (supply) and at the same time as those related to the differentiated behaviour of the clientele

---

[7]    Data 2002 drawn from www.fipe.it "Evoluzione degli stili alimentari negli ultimi anni" (Evolution of eating habits in recent years)

[8]    Considerations drawn from www.fipe.it "Evoluzione degli stili alimentari negli ultimi anni" and from Maria del Duca – Emanuela Schiaffella, Una proposta gestionale per l'impresa ristorativi (A management Proposal for Food Service Businesses), in Ricette della cucina italiana per la ristorazione programmata a menu rotativi (Italian Recipes for Food Service Planned with Rotating Menues), in collaboration with FIPE, Franco Angeli, Milan, Italy, 1995

(demand)[9]. There have been, and still are, numerous attempts, not always successful, to apply at least the principles at the basis of revenue management systems to small and medium size hospitality businesses: in the European market, the prevalence of the SMEs obstructs the spread of such systems both for objective reasons (size barriers) and for reasons tied to the entrepreneurial culture (managerial barriers) [10].

Despite this, studies and research progress at a rapid pace: in the last five-year period, besides developments in the "traditional" themes such as, for example, forecasting models and models for managing the capacity to supply a service, researchers have gone in depth into the application of systems of revenue management in food service businesses, thanks to the contributions of the American school[11], which has stimulated studies and research applied to a sector considered, in the past, "uninteresting" and lacking organisational models and models of advanced management processes.

---

[9]  E. Schiaffella, "Yield Management in albergo: alcuni modelli di gestione della capacità ricettiva" (Yield Management in the hotle: some models for managing lodging capacity), in Turistica, vol. 1, 1999, page 71 and following.; P. Desinano, M. S. Minuti, E. Schiaffella, F. Sfodera, "Issues regarding yield management in the hospitality industry - New directions for research", proceedings of the Fourth Annual International Yield & Revenue Management Conference, 5-7 September 1999, Colchester Insitute, Centre for Management Studies; M. Berretta, P. Desinano, M. S. Minuti, E. Schiaffella, F. Sfodera, "Yield Management - Uno strumento innovativo per la gestione dei ricavi nelle imprese turistiche" (Yield Management – An innovative instrument for revenue management in tourism businesses), Economia & Management, n. 2, March, 2000, pag. 73

[10]  European Commission - Directorate General XXIII - Tourism Unit, Yield Management in small and medium sized enterprises in the tourist industry, 1996.

[11]  Sheryl E. Kimes, Richard B, Chase, Sunmee Choi, Elizabeth N. Ngonzi, Phillip Y. Lee, Restaurant Revenue Management, Cornell Hotel and Restaurant Administration Quarterly, 1998, 40-3, pages 18-30; Sheryl E. Kimes, Deborah I. Barrash, John E. Alexander, Developing a restaurant revenue management strategy, Cornell Hotel and Restaurant Administration Quarterly, 1999, 34-5, pages 18-30; Sheryl E. Kimes, Jochen Wirtz, Perceived fairness of demand based pricing for restaurants, Cornell Hotel and Restaurant Administration Quarterly, 2002, 41-1, pages 31-38; Sheryl E. Kimes, Jochen Wirtz,Breffni M. Noone, How long should dinner take? Measuring expected duration for restaurant revenue management, Cornell University School of Hotel Administration, working paper 11-04-2002; Sheryl E. Kimes, Gary M. Thompson, An evaluation of heuristic method for determining the best table mix in full service restaurants, Cornell University School of Hotel Administration, working paper 09-01-2002; Sheryl E. Kimes, Gary M. Thompson, Restaurant Revenue Management at Chevvs: determining the best table mix, Cornell University School of Hotel Administration, working paper 07-05-2002

### 2.1.2 Applicability requirements and food service businesses

Food service businesses have all the requirements for the application of revenue management systems:

1. *Fixed supply capacity*
   Since the objective of revenue management is the efficient allocation of capacity, the systems cannot be applied where capacity is able to adjust rapidly to the demand, using the example of stock. When the supply capacity is variable, and not very expensive, it is possible to increase or decrease it to meet the variations in the demand. The rigidity of production capacity represents a critical factor for a business, not only in managing the high points of variable demand, but also the moments of low demand, especially where general fixed costs have considerable impact.
2. *Perishable products and/or services with the passage of time*
   Food service is perishable with the passage of time: an empty table generates a loss of revenue which can never be recuperated.
   The closer one gets to the moment of the presumed sale, the less value an unsold table has: once the variable cost is covered, any revenue is better than none. The crucial point of revenue management is to avoid selling at reduced prices, when it is possible to sell at higher prices; in the same way, a service must not remain unsold because of prices that are too high for the clientele that requests it.
3. *Variable demand*
   Restaurateurs undergo demand oscillations on various levels: seasonal variations are affected by the habits and consumption behaviours of the demand; weekly variations are created by different types of demand that use the service; daily variations depend on any events and manifestations located near the structure. Revenue management attempts to "flatten" the demand peaks, by manoeuvring prices and the strategic alternatives of marketing.
4. *Demand which can be segmented*
   The demand must be able to be segmented in a clear and precise manner, so that it is possible to develop a differentiated pricing strategy, in order to separate clients willing, and able, to pay higher prices, from those who will change their habits to obtain lower prices. It is important that the segments, and therefore the prices, be completely independent, in order to avoid a dilution of prices caused by the passage of clients from one segment to another.
5. *Stochastic demand*
   Revenue management deals with dynamic variables and uncertain variables: there is uncertainty about the number of reservations requested by each market segment and about the reservation dates; the dynamism is inherent in the fact that there is an evolution of the reservations over time, decreasing or increasing, according to the type of clients, and in function of this the allocations of tables left are reviewed daily.

6. *Product that can be sold in advance*
   Food service can be sold in advance and, other important factor, market segments demonstrated different behaviour characteristics in making reservations.

7. *Price-sensitive demand*
   Market segments, according to revenue management logic, must have a different price sensitivity; in other words, one must be able to influence the demand with pricing manoeuvres which, from time to time, the system sets moving to meet market conditions.

8. *Low marginal sales costs and high fixed production costs*
   If there is availability, the sale of a supplementary table entails sustaining low costs, mostly tied to variable costs. Inversely, if there is no availability, there are high production costs which impede the satisfaction of a supplementary service request, because of the fixed capacity, at least in the short term, of the food service business.

## 2.2 Revenue management and Italian food service businesses: application difficulties

### 2.2.1 Structural limits

As mentioned previously, the Italian food service sector is characterised by a high level of fragmentation of businesses, in which the presence of small companies prevails, not infrequently characterised by managerial, organisational and structural systems that are by now obsolete. Small dimensions are not suited to revenue management: the studies applied, reported in foreign publications, deal with much vaster dimensions: 230-240 seats[12]. In the Italian context this is applicable *tout court* in very few cases; in most structures only the principles that inspire revenue management systems (which can concern the management of tariffs and of reservations ) can be applied.

Moreover, there is the problem of the scanty computerisation of Italian food service structures; approximately 65% of the companies (excluding those included in institutional food service) are without computer equipment sufficient to elaborate and manage data coming from outside the firm and which are essential to understand the environmental situation in which they are obliged to operate. "...*A yield management system is a high intensity information system and this elects information technology to a key role in its management. In fact, each phase*

---

[12] Sheryl E. Kimes, Gary M. Thompson, An evaluation of heuristic method for determining the best table mix in full service restaurants, Cornell University School of Hotel Administration, op. cit.; Sheryl E. Kimes, Gary M. Thompson, Restaurant Revenue Management at Chevvs: determining the best table mix, Cornell University School of Hotel Administration, op. cit.

*of the process consumes data and produces information. The availability of detailed data on the demand, addressing the company in digital format, that is, such to permit its computerised elaboration is an essential requirement in implementing a yield management system. The companies which adopted information systems earliest are those which potentially can realistically implement an authentic yield management system ..."* [13] It is totally evident that without adequate computerisation the gathering and elaboration of data is not possible for:

- demand segmentation
- demand forecasting
- the definition and allocation of production capacity
- the sale of services.

## 2.2.2  Managerial limitations

The size factor strongly affects the management of a firm: besides a de-structured or inexistent wide-spread innovation process, the Italian food service sector has difficulty finding resources dedicated to the research and development of new product lines, to marketing, to management control, but it especially suffers from a tendential absence of an entrepreneurial culture oriented towards innovation, also in virtue of the fact that the sector does not present elevated "entry barriers"; therefore it is crowded with competitors, often not adequately prepared not only in the area of professional techniques but also in the operational - managerial area.

Management "by exception", or hands-on management, represents one of the sector's weaknesses: the concepts of market segmentation, positioning, marketing, market target, forecasting, and production capacity management are therefore not always compatible with the broad managerial scheme in which Italian firms operate.

Therefore it is above all the managerial gap which obstructs the spread of revenue management systems in the Italian food service sector: overcoming this will be a long and complex journey, in which, however, the examples are not lacking of coherent management with the high-level laws and ways of being of industrialisation, unionisation and economic development reached by the nation.

---

[13]  M. Berretta, P. Desinano, M. S. Minuti, E. Schiaffella, F. Sfodera, "Yield Management - Uno strumento innovativo per la gestione dei ricavi nelle imprese turistiche" (Yield Management – An innovative instrument for revenue management in tourism businesses), Economia & Management, n. 2, March, 2000, page 73

# Recent events, challenges and options in revenue management

**Paolo Desinano**

p.desinano@cstassisi,it

CST – Università di Perugia

Via C. Cecci, 1 – 06088 – Assisi (PG) – Italy

*Contents: 1 Introduction. 2 Y&RM community: towards growing consolidation. 3 CRM vs. Y&RM? 4 The spreading fascination of RM. 5 Conclusions. References*

## 1  Introduction

During the four years since the Assisi Conference on Yield and Revenue Management (Y&RM) many events have changed the vision and perceptions on this topic. The crisis of the web economy, well analysed by Porter (2001), is only one of the events that have characterised this period (I do not want to discuss the September 11 tragedy and its heavy consequences for the tourist industry).

The aim of this brief paper is to point out some emerging issues that pose new challenges to Y&RM theory and practice.

A first important issue is the growing consolidation of the scientific debate on the topic. Two fundamental tools have been very useful in that structuring. The first is the publication of the "Journal of Revenue and Pricing Management" starting in the Spring of 2002. The second important event is the new edition of Ingold and Yeoman's seminal book with McMahon as co-editor (Ingold, McMahon-Beattie and Yeoman, 2000). It is very important that the Y&RM scholar and practitioner community have access to specific tools to <u>better</u> perform their work.

On the side of new challenges there are, among others, at least two interesting and problematical topics related to Y&RM: the adoption of e-CRM systems and a demand driven supply approach.

In this paper a paragraph is dedicated to each of the issues cited. A final paragraph draws some brief conclusions.

## 2   Y&RM community: towards growing consolidation

In the last three decades the Y&RM community has been part of the larger OR (Operations Research) community. Most important papers were published in journals such as *Interfaces*, *Management Science* and so on. These journals deal with strictly technical topics but Y&RM is a complex topic that cannot be reduced to mathematical programming or statistics. In fact, a Y&RM system implementation implies consequences at various organisational levels from human resources (i.e. personnel training) to marketing management (i.e. price and fare fairness and/or customer loyalty) and so on. Up to now this broader approach found expression in special interest groups related to specific sectors (i.e. AGIFORS of IATA and similar).

In this context the "Journal of Revenue and Pricing Management" fills a gap. Henry Stewart Publications in London began publishing the Journal in the Spring of 2002. The journal's organisation, using three regional editors, offers a large geographical coverage. Furthermore the special space dedicated to practical papers permits a interesting comparison with real business experience and non academic authors. This innovative format allows a fruitful deployment of Y&RM studies, approaches and techniques.

In 1987 Yeoman and Ingold edited an important book on Y&RM that covered the most important related topics. The book received wide acceptance and three years later the two editors, with the important addition of Una McMahon, published the second edition of the work. The new book contains twenty-one papers as opposed to the fourteen papers of the first edition. Also the authors increased from twenty to twenty-nine and the pages from 248 to 346. These figures reveal that RM philosophy is extending its influence towards new and wider horizons. In particular the application domain has been extended to include cruise, restaurant and football businesses.

## 3   CRM vs. Y&RM?

"Customer retention" is an imperative that must always be observed in tourism businesses. The hotel guest history system is one of the most popular technological implementations of that imperative. It is unthinkable to apply the same fare rules to new customer as to repeat clients. Faced with these alternatives we must reason in two different ways, in other words, there are two different revenue optimisation domains: one for repeaters and one for new clients. The company marketing policy must decide about the reciprocal weight of each domain. In the end the new central question is: is it wiser to seek immediate profitable returns or a long-term relation in which the customer repeats his/her purchase?

Relationship marketing is the basis for developing durable and attractive relations with one's own customers. In (McCaskey, 1998) and (Noone and Griffin, 1998) a possible conflict was pointed out between Y&RM and the relationship marketing approach. This question was also mentioned in (Desinano et al., 1999). The issue is important because it affects two technical aspects where revenues can be maximised: the time horizon (how many nights?) and inventory capacity (how many rooms?).

A new issue called "customer relationship management" (CRM) can be added to these aspects. Since the 1990's CRM has become a central theme in management studies and practices. The CRM approach requires a more complex evaluation of the customer's value and makes feasibility studies on Y&RM adoption more difficult. Will CRM cause the death of classical Y&RM, or is it the next evolutionary step of Y&RM?

Furthermore an important organisational issue emerges: can an organisation trained for YM sustain a CRM policy? Is the Y&RM-oriented business culture compatible with a CRM-oriented one?

If one-to-one marketing kills segmentation (Rayport and Jaworsky, 2001) one of the classical foundations of Y&RM disappears. These questions may seem extreme, nevertheless this is a time of profound changes. Our theory must be corroborated and well founded.

# 4   The spreading fascination of RM

The theoretical principles of Y&RM are well known. (Kimes, 1989) is the most frequently cited reference. These principles are generally accepted by the Y&RM community. The association between capacity-constrained production and the service firm is almost automatic. In 1998 Schwartz discussed and criticised the well-known foundations of Y&RM. On this basis it could seem strange that Manugistics Inc. acquired Talus in the last quarter of 2000. Indeed Manugistics is the leading software house for manufacturing systems while Talus, in turn, is a leader in RM systems. What happened?

In the past decade re-engineering in many manufacturing companies has driven managers and consultants to develop and deploy new production models; many of these were inspired by the JIT approach. It is particularly important to integrate production processes to include logistic ones, both inbound and outbound (Poirer, 1999). Supply chain management (SCM) or Supply chain automation (SCA) are typical expressions that refer to this vision of which the well known "zero inventory" concept is part. This concept is valid for both inbound (raw materials) and outbound (final products) inventory. Operating under those assumptions yet another concept, the "demand driven supply" concept, is derived; with this system the supply is activated and controlled "on demand", i.e. upon the customers' orders.

In effect "zero inventory" is equivalent to the "fixed capacity" assumption of Y&RM. But that is not the only assumption that new manufacturing organisations share with the Y&RM approach. With the end of mass production (Pine, 1993) manufacturing firms are also compelled to tackle a highly segmented and time varied demand to the limit of 1:1 relations (Peppers and Rogers, 1990). In this situation the ability to perform reliable forecasting of customer behaviour becomes a key competency of the firm. To be able to analyse historical demand and recognise patterns has become a fundamental skill for the leading enterprises of many industries not just service ones. Y&RM techniques can extend their application domain beyond traditional boundaries (Secomandi et al., 2002).

These brief considerations show that new trends are emerging which can profoundly modify deep-rooted ways of buying, producing, selling and distributing. The traditional theories must also be reviewed and reformulated.

# 5 Conclusions

The pioneer period of yield management developed from the 1970s to 1990s. I call this period YM 1.0. In this period Yield management grew from its first empirical and practical applications to more recent and sophisticated techniques to finally become a systematic and rigorous discipline in management studies. A specific segment of software systems was developed and many tools are available for the companies that intend to embrace this approach. The Y&RM scholar and practitioner community is well established and equipped with its own specific tools such as journals, books, courses, conferences etc.

Recent business developments delineate new scenarios, at first glance not completely compatible with classic Y&RM assumptions. While the e-CRM approach would suggest a new look at the concept of "fairness" (Kimes, 1994). "Demand driven production" in manufacturing seeks to extend the traditional domain of Y&RM applications. Perhaps we need a YM 2.0 version that extends beyond traditional application domains. The Y&RM practitioner and scholar community is asked to take up the challenge toward new and exciting applications in ever changing business scenarios.

# References

Desinano P., M.S. Minuti, E. Schiaffella, F. Sfodera, *Issues regarding yield management applications in the hospitality industry. New directions for research*, Proceedings of the 4th Annual International Yield Management Conference, Clacton Campus, Colchester (UK), 1999.

Ingold A., U. McMahon-Beattie, I Yeoman (eds), *Yield Management. Strategies for the Service Industries*. 2nd edition, Continuum, London, 2000.

Kimes S.E., *The Basics of Yield Management*, The Cornell H.R.A. Quarterly, November, Vol. 30, No. 3, 14-19, 1989.

Kimes S.E., *Perceived Fairness of Yield Management*, The Cornell H.R.A. Quarterly, February, Vol. 35, No. 1, 1994, pp. 22-29.

McCaskey D., *Yield management vs relationship marketing*, Proceedings of the 3rd Annual International Yield Management Conference, University of Ulster, Portrush (UK), 1998.

Noone B., P. Griffin, *Managing the long-term profit yield from market segments in a hotel environment: a case study on the implementation of customer profitability analysis*, Proceedings of the 3rd Annual International Yield Management Conference, University of Ulster, Portrush (UK), 1998.

Peppers D., M. Rogers, *The One to One Future: Building Relationships One Customer at a Time*, Currency Doubleday, New York, 1993.

Pine II, B., *Mass Customization: The New Frontier in Business Competition*, Harvard Business School Press, Boston, 1993.

Poirer C., *Advanced Supply Chain Management*, Barrett-Koelher Publishers, S. Francisco, 1999.

Porter M.E., *Strategy and the Internet*, Harvard Business Review, March, 2001, pp. 63-78.

Rayport J.F., B.J. Jaworsky , *e-Commerce*, Mc-Graw-Hill, New York, 2001.

Schwartz Z., *The Confusing Side of Yield Management: Myths, Errors, and Misconceptions*, Journal of Hospitality & Tourism Research, vol. 22, No. 4, 1998, pp. 413-30.

Secomandi N., K. Abbott, T. Atan, E.A. Boyd, *From Revenue Management Concepts to Software Systems*, Interfaces, vol. 32, No. 2, March-April, 2002, pp. 1-11.

Yeoman I, A. Ingold (eds), *Yield Management. Strategies for the Service Industries*, Cassell, London, 1997.

# Part III

# Information instruments for a YMS in the hospitality industry

# Microsoft Fidelio: Opus 2 overview

## Opus 2 Revenue Technologies

7031 Columbia Gateway Drive
Columbia, MD 21046-2289
United States of America

*Contents: 1 Organisation & scope of operations. 1.1 Service/product overview. 2 Supplier's description of goods and services. 2.1 System architecture. 2.2 Property configuration. 2.3 Property initialization. 2.4 Data flow. 3 RMS system versions. 3.1 Interfaces. 3.2 Forecasting. 3.2.1 History sets. 3.2.2 Trending. 3.2.3 Hourly reforecasting. 3.2.4 Forecastable clusters. 3.2.5 Special events/demand changes. 4 Group management.*

# 1   Organisation & scope of operations

Originally established in 1985 as Eric B. Orkin Associates, Inc., the company became OPUS 2 Revenue Technologies, Inc. (OPUS 2) in 1992 and a wholly owned subsidiary of MICROS Systems, Inc. on October 1, 1999. Our corporate office is located in Portsmouth, New Hampshire with a field office located in San Francisco, California. The company's continued success is based on a commitment to providing clients with strategies, technology and training to achieve and surpass revenue goals.

The principals of OPUS 2 have a hospitality industry record of high achievement from combining hotel leadership in operations and marketing with revenue management and computer software expertise. At the core of system development is a team of MIS professionals truly operating at the forefront of PC-based systems, client-server technology and applications development.

A complementary staff of consultants and trainers drawn from hospitality backgrounds has gained acknowledgement for OPUS 2 as a provider of creative, effective and highly motivational training.

The knowledge gained through years of research and practical problem solving in the revenue management area underpins the ultimate system solution for your company and reduces the risks associated with implementation.

Our core business areas are development of both yield management and yield based central reservation systems for the hospitality industry. Installed in over 250 properties worldwide, our initial TopLine yield management system has become our legacy. In 1995, we successfully deployed a new paradigm reservation system for Outrigger Hotels. TopLine PROPHET, a Windows-based, fully automated hotel yield management system was initially launched in 1996. As a successor to the popular TopLine system, TopLine PROPHET has already been chosen by over 300 hotels including though not limited to the following:

- Starwood Hotels and Resorts.

- Swissôtel at worldwide locations.

- Sunburst Hotels (Choice Hotels).

- Boca Raton Resort & Club.

- La Quinta Resort & Spa.

- Hershey Lodge and Convention Center.

- Caesar's World.

- Grupo Posadas Hotels throughout Mexico.

- Greenalls Hotels & Leisure Limited.

- Cok Hotels, Amsterdam.

- Colonial Williamsburg.

- MGM Grand.

OPUS 2 is exceptionally sound financially and operationally with steady growth in employees, clients and sales. We undertake consulting and development projects in a disciplined manner and take pride in our innovative software applications with clean, easy-to-use interfaces that have become our hallmark and the basis for a high level of customer satisfaction.

OPUS 2 is a wholly owned subsidiary of MICROS® Systems, Inc. of Beltsville, Maryland.

## 1.1 Service/product overview

OPUS 2 has taken a leading role in the development of yield management systems. The two most widely installed products are TopLine and TopLine PROPHET.

TopLine was initially introduced in 1985. Since then, it has been installed in over 250 properties around the world.

The system has evolved over the years, continually revised and enhanced on a regular maintenance schedule. The current matured version is 3.10.

TopLine PROPHET (TLP) was released in 1996. It is a comprehensive Yield Management package. Since its introduction, over 300 hotels have selected TLP. TopLine PROPHET provides:

1. Maximization of transient revenue through sophisticated forecasting and optimization.

2. Maximization of group revenue via detailed analysis of group business provided via a real-time interface to your sales and catering system or via our own group booking module.

3. Incentive systems to influence sales managers and reservation agents to produce the most revenue for your hotels.

Other features include:

• TLP automatically implements optimal settings and provides management with a master control panel for viewing the solutions and modifying them if needed;

• TLP provides tools for all market segments: leisure, conventions, meetings, contract accounts and others. Profit contributions from all revenue streams are considered, as is displacement of short lead-time business when making longer lead-time decisions.

Version 3.5 of TopLine PROPHET is currently deployed. Version 4.00 with an expected release in the first quarter of 2000 will include enhancements to increase the client interface functionality as well as a Global Distribution System (GDS) optimization report. OPUS 2 is in the development phases of design for TopLine PROPHET Enterprise, a solution to allow easy access to a centrally installed version of TopLine PROPHET via internet, extranet and intranet.

OPUS 2 takes the lead role in the planning, implementation and rollout of yield management products.

# 2 Supplier's description of goods and services

The responses provided in this section refer to a scenario that would involve either a CRS or PMS solution.

## 2.1 System architecture

TopLine PROPHET was developed using Delphi from Inprise, an object-oriented Pascal language development environment and compiler, which runs under Windows NT, Windows 95, or Windows 98 operating systems on Intel-based PCs. Decision support servers are recommended to be 300MHz Pentium II PCs with

128MB RAM and a 1GB hard drive. The database server can be a similar PC with dual 4GB hard drives or any reasonably powerful Unix machine. The database system used is Oracle. TCP/IP is required as a communications protocol. Only a licensed copy of the database engine software is required in addition to the operating system and the application.

## 2.2 Property configuration

Individual room types within the PMS/CRS are easily cross-referenced or mapped to room types within TopLine PROPHET. The cluster concept in TopLine PROPHET allows the hotel to group room types with similar demand patterns so they may be forecasted independently. TopLine PROPHET supports a 'Run of House' room type.

TopLine PROPHET controls rate availability by rate values rather than by rate type, therefore, there is no need to map PMS/CRS rate types to our system.

Local and Preferred Account business may be treated differently than normal FIT business by using the TopLine PROPHET concepts of 'indifference rate' and/or 'yieldability'. An 'indifference rate' may be assigned to Local and Preferred Accounts that allows them to remain open when equivalent FIT rates are closed. Assigning a 'yieldability' status of non-yieldable will keep Local and Preferred Account rates open under all circumstances.

TopLine PROPHET's ability to store historical data or future inventory is limited only by the disk space available to the TLP database. If at the time of an installation, historical data is available from the PMS/CRS the amount of data loaded into TopLine PROPHET may vary on a property by property basis.

The amount of future inventory held in TopLine PROPHET may be configured by each property.

TopLine PROPHET does not currently support any configuration at the brand level though this feature could be easily added if required.

## 2.3 Property initialization

Several pieces of data are needed in order to initialize the TopLine PROPHET database. As long as the required historical data exists in the PMS/CRS, it may be imported directly from these systems into TopLine PROPHET. For an opening hotel, or one with very little relevant history, the data must be entered manually. Combining historical data from a PMS/CRS with manual estimates entered by the user is also possible.

Although a hotel may have five years of history, it may not be appropriate to load all of this data into TopLine PROPHET, as changing market conditions may render some of the data irrelevant. During the initialization process, we can choose to import reservation records from a certain period of time, thus avoiding periods of data that do not accurately reflect the current market conditions for this hotel. In the case of a new hotel, where historical data is not available the required data is entered manually. With the assistance of an OPUS 2 Consultant, market conditions will be reviewed with the hotel's management team in order to determine basic data for the property. The understanding is that although this data is the initial "seed" used by TopLine PROPHET for forecasting, the system will immediately begin to adjust as real transactions are accepted from the PMS/CRS and actual history is created. See Section 3.2 for a discussion of Bayesian learning model.

New hotels with or without heavy seasonality go through the same initialization process. During our discussions, seasonality is addressed so that a set of data will be developed for each season. See Section 3.2.A for a discussion of History Sets.

When historical data is imported from the PMS/CRS and it does not coincide with management's opinions, the following will be reviewed: Step one is to understand why management disagrees with this historical data.

The data could be correct, but management's perceptions may in fact be incorrect. If after further investigation it is determined that although the historical data is correct it does not reflect future trends, management can make manual overrides to the historical "seed". Thus, there is a high degree of flexibility allowed when configuring TopLine PROPHET.

During the initialization and configuration of TopLine PROPHET we can load some data from the PMS/CRS as listed in Section 2.4, Data Flow. There is also some data that must be configured directly into TopLine PROPHET. This data includes, but is not limited to:

- history set dates;
- market segments;
- account information;
- users;
- room types;
- group pricing strategies;
- transient pricing strategies;
- yieldability;
- indifference rate;
- group Potential;
- oversell allowances;

134

- upgrade Levels;
- rate gaps;
- report Parameters.

Figure 1

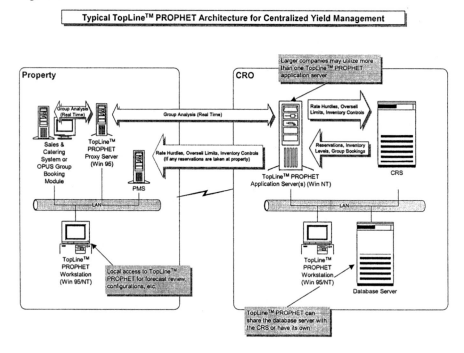

**Typical TopLine™ PROPHET Architecture for Centralized Yield Management**

## 2.4 Data flow

On a nightly basis, TopLine PROPHET reforecasts and re-optimises as far into the future as the long-term planning horizon. In addition, the application re-optimises the near-term, on a more frequent basis. For these reasons, we recommend nightly updates of all data from the CRS combined with hourly updates of reservations data. TLP supports user requests for data updates as well as the manual initiation of the optimization process for future dates if a significant event warrants this action. Currently, we do not update based upon a certain amount of activity though a future release will support event-driven updates. TopLine PROPHET also has these data types available, inventory, both physical and off-market, and by room type. Inventory and Group Bookings are passed nightly. Reservation transactions can be passed as frequently as hourly.

The data is stored in tables in the RMS database. Additional data types available are Stay Pattern Rate Hurdles and Inventory Controls. Data required by the PMS/CRS that has changed as a result of recalculation by TopLine PROPHET is passed to the PMS/CRS immediately.

# 3 RMS system versions

Version 3.50 of TopLine PROPHET is currently deployed. Version 4.00 is currently in alpha testing. In addition, we are in the early stages of the design of TopLine PROPHET Enterprise. This product will allow access to a centralized installation of TopLine PROPHET via internet, extranet or intranet. It will feature a browser-based client that will bring the full power of TopLine PROPHET to any desktop while minimizing deployment and support issues. Version 3.50 contains enhanced processing and analysis of group bookings. The application will support multiple group types (e.g., wholesale, base business, true groups) with a unique analysis for each type.

Version 4.00 increases the functionality of the client interface, as well as providing a GDS optimization report. Version 3.50 was released in the first quarter of 1999 and version 4.00 is currently expected to be released in the first quarter of 2000. Subsequent versions will be released on a semi-annual basis.

## 3.1 Interfaces

TopLine PROPHET currently interfaces to the following vendors:

- Choice Hotels (Profit Manager) PMS.
- GEAC Computers PMS.
- Hotel Computers (INNtime) PMS.
- Hotel Information Systems PMS.
- MICROS Fidelio PMS and SCS.
- Visual One (formerly National Guest Systems) (Miracle III) SCS.
- Springer Miller (Host) PMS.
- Eltrax (LANmark) PMS.
- TCA (INNSIST) PMS.
- Inter American Data (LMS) PMS.

Additional interfaces are currently being developed with the following vendors:

- Newmarket Software (Delphi for Windows) SCS.
- Rio Systems PMS.
- National Guest Systems (IS4VB) PMS.
- National Guest Systems (Visual Miracle) SCS.
- Daylight Software SCS.
- Eltrax (Medallion) PMS.

OPUS 2 has had discussions with additional PMS and CRS vendors. As those agreements are finalized the interfaces will be developed.

## 3.2 Forecasting

TopLine PROPHET uses a Bayesian statistical model for forecasting all the variables of interest (e.g., transient booking pace). The Bayesian model has numerous advantages over traditional "frequentist" statistical techniques such as time series analysis. The Bayesian school of statistics is based on a different view of what it means to learn from data.

In the more traditional frequentist approaches probability is a property of the event itself and is used to explain the phenomenon. The Bayesian model uses probability as a measure of uncertainty about the phenomenon. As actual data on the variables is accumulated, the distributions are updated in a manner that adapts based on the degree and consistency of deviation from the prior distributions. In this way, no arbitrary weights or smoothing need be applied to the data.

Another advantage of the Bayesian model is the ability to combine subjective estimates with objective information to generate a prior distribution that then gets modified by actual history to produce a new posterior distribution. Estimates or actual data that were once reasonable but are unsupported by more recent data are automatically modelled as less likely to occur in the future. This allows TopLine PROPHET to be successfully installed in a hotel with no available history or one that is experiencing rapid market change and still receive immediate benefit.

All distributions in TopLine PROPHET are of unconstrained behavior. When actual observed data is constrained or censored by a rate hurdle or inventory restriction, data augmentation algorithms are used to calculate the effect of the missing data on the distributions.

This approach is far more accurate than using "regret" and "denial" from a subset of reservation distribution channels.

### 3.2.1 History sets

TopLine PROPHET uses History Sets to associate past and future days in a predictive relationship. The assignment of days to particular history sets is a simple point and click on a calendar operation. There is no limit on the number of history sets. Past or future days may be reassigned at any time. In this way a day may be moved from the "High Season" set to the "Convention – Overflow Hotel" set as soon as a citywide convention is announced. This is an infinitely flexible approach for handling all types of market conditions.

### 3.2.2  Trending

Prior to the availability of actual data for a future day, TopLine PROPHET uses distributions from its assigned history set to forecast future demand, rate distributions, stay patterns, etc. As actual reservations and cancellations occur for the day deviations from the expected behaviour are trended with the prior estimate to generate a revised forecast.

### 3.2.3  Hourly reforecasting

Reforecasting and subsequent re-optimisation occurs regularly throughout the day (e.g., hourly) for short lead times (e.g., next fourteen days). This is vitally important for establishments with walk-in volume or volatile transient demand. Longer lead time dates (from a transient standpoint) are reforecasted and re-optimised on a daily basis.

### 3.2.4  Forecastable clusters

TopLine PROPHET allows the user to configure the hotel's room types into separate forecastable clusters. This is useful when a hotel has room types of widely different desirability and therefore experiences significant differences in demand. An example is an oceanfront hotel that can run 100% occupancy in the rooms with a view while achieving 75% in the rest of the hotel.

TopLine PROPHET automatically compares actual data to forecasts and makes appropriate adjustments.

Graphic comparisons of actual data to forecast data demonstrate the accuracy of the history set in forecasting the particular day.

TopLine PROPHET features automatic outlier detection as well as the ability to manually override a day's outlier status.

Once a day has passed, its data is compared with all like days in the history set to determine its degree of consistency. If it is found to be deviant in any of the significant distributions, the day is tagged by TopLine PROPHET as an outlier and its data is not included in calculation of history set forecasts. Each time a day of the week (e.g., Sunday) is processed, all like days are reanalyzed for deviance. In this way, a new trend in the data will cause older days to be tagged as outliers and more recent days to be untagged. All outlier tags can be overridden by the user.

User entered forecast overrides are shown graphically in comparison to the system forecast. In addition, the Overrides report shows all overrides, their values, and the current system value. TopLine PROPHET continues to update its forecast but does not override the user-entered change. An Audit report shows all changes and the user who made them.

### 3.2.5 Special events/demand changes

Patterns of behaviour that are extraordinary and will never happen again such as hurricanes, disasters, and renovations are demand periods that are designated as 'outliers' in TopLine PROPHET. These dates are not included in the historical data that is used for forecast purposes therefore the database will not be infected with information that has no bearing on future dates. TopLine PROPHET automatically detects 'outliers', or they can be manually entered and overridden by the user.

If a change in demand patterns such as a sudden economic surge causing business to trend upward would indicate that a new history set should be created to reflect the increase in demand, or if the change has been consistent over the last few weeks, then this data can be used to create a new history set that will be used from this point forward. A new history set would thus be created using this recent data and would involve minimal intervention from the user.

## 4  Group management

TopLine PROPHET fully yield manages both group and transient segments. In order to fully determine the appropriate rate hurdles for each arrival date and length of stay of the transient guest, it is assumed that the entire demand "picture" is taken into consideration. Thus the groups play an important role in this process.

Group business can be entered directly into TopLine PROPHET or via an interface to the Sales and Catering system (see section 1.7 Interfaces). Either method will provide the Sales Manager with a comprehensive analysis of the group's profitability to the hotel.

The group is assigned a Booking Point value, which measures the profitability of the group in relation to the market position of the hotel during the requested dates. It will also measure the impact this group will have on any lost transient revenue. In order to do this, TopLine PROPHET considers all revenue sources for the group (Rooms, F&B, function room rental, etc) as well as costs (Incremental costs, commissions, rebates, comp rooms, etc).

This data is compared against the Lose It rate for the time period as well as the transient revenue displacement in order to obtain a Booking Point value. TopLine PROPHET will also advise the Sales Manager of any alternative arrival dates that may be more profitable for the hotel.

In regards to transient optimization, all near term days and their stay patterns are optimized on an hourly basis. All future stay patterns are optimized on a nightly basis. These are configured for each property individually. Likewise, the user can manually initiate the optimization of future dates if a significant event warrants such an action. A future version of TopLine PROPHET will allow for the automatic initiation of the transient optimization based on a major change in demand. The transient rate hurdle values and stay pattern controls that are generated due to the optimization process can all be modified by the user if need be.

# e-yield™ technical brief

## IDeaS Inc., Integrating Decisions and Systems

3500 Yankee Drive, Suite 350
Eagan, MN 55121, USA

## 1  e-yield™

### 1.1  What is e-yield™?

E-yield integrates hotel management expertise and IDeaS statistical market models into optimal revenue decisions. The combination of **Full Precision Forecasting**, The **e-yield Decision Engine** and **Decision Integration** create a powerful system that delivers on the 4% guarantee: *We will increase revenues by at least 4% (above and beyond market forces) for all room inventory impacted by the e-yield Solution. In addition, the system will deliver significant benefits to the hotels with modules such as group evaluation, contract evaluation, management information, monitoring and many more.*

What are the Components of e-yield™?

| Component | Description |
|---|---|
| Historical Data Capture | Raw data is collected from the PMS/CRS (property management system or central reservation system) history file and snapshots of current databases are taken. No other system comes close to e-yield in historical data capture or usage. |

| Component | Description |
|---|---|
| Data Analysis, Verification and Calibration | The historical data is analyzed for patterns and exceptions. e-yield extracts the following: booking pace, demand patterns (length-of-stay, day-of-week, no-shows, cancellations and seasonality) and special events. Hotel management works with IDeaS yield professionals to configure the system. |
| e-yield Data | This includes detailed, summary and configuration data for e-yield. |
| e-yield Decision Integration | e-yield integrates seamlessly with the PMS/CRS to implement hotel management strategy. It provides the PMS/CRS with the overbooking and opportunity cost information needed to automatically determine availability based on rate and length-of-stay requested. e-yield also extracts information necessary to monitor forecasts and update controls from the PMS/CRS databases. |
| Full Precision Forecast | Forecasts are prepared using demand patterns and the corresponding uncertainty, special event databases, on-books information and user demand changes. Unconstrained forecasts (not limited to the capacity of the hotel) are prepared for each of the following: demand, no-show and cancellation, booking pace and rate. |
| e-yield Decision Engine | Opportunity cost is the expected revenue generated from the last available room. It is calculated based on the demand forecasts and used to make rate and length-of-stay decisions. The e-yield Decision Engine calculates opportunity cost, then writes this data directly to the hotel PMS/CRS. Opportunity cost includes non-room revenue and cost factors to allow hotels to maximize revenue per customer, not just revenues per room. This module also includes overbooking controls that are configured to meet hotel management's risk vs. benefit strategy. It allows "overbooking" to make up for slippage or "wash" due to no-shows, cancellations or early departures. |
| PMS/CRS Data | These are databases the PMS/CRS read from and write to. |

| Component | Description |
|---|---|
| PMS/CRS | This is the property management system or central reservation system. |
| Updating | PMS/CRS data is extracted nightly and is used to update the e-yield database. This allows the system to make daily adjustments for changes in market behaviour. |
| Monitoring | The monitoring module compares on-books data with data from the current forecast. Significant deviations are noted as exceptions. |
| e-yield GUI | This is the e-yield graphical user interface. It provides the screens necessary for hotel management to interact with the program. |
| Calendar | Significant deviations of on-books data from the forecast are identified via the calendar. Exception dates are identified in red to alert hotel management. |
| Group Evaluation | A tool that helps the group sales manager evaluate a group based on profitability, placement, displaced transient demand and fair market rate. |
| Reports | Tabular and graphical reports that help hotel management analyze a dynamic marketplace. |
| Demand Change | A module in the e-yield GUI that allows hotel management to override the system. Use of this module is encouraged only in cases where the system will not be able to respond to demand changes in time. |
| Hotel Management | This group consists of hotel management personnel that interact with the yield management system. |
| IDeaS Yield Professionals | Hoteliers, mathematicians, scientists and engineers employed by IDeaS. They partner with hotel management to help set optimum yield strategy, address problems and answer questions. |

## 1.2 Why e-yield™?

The **Full Precision Forecast** is a revolutionary statistical approach to forecasting demand and the corresponding uncertainty. It is conducted at a level of detail not found in any other system. The forecast is produced by properly interpreting benchmark rates, occupancy trends, out of order rooms, market segmentation, day of week patterns, length-of-stay patterns, historical and future block activity, booking pace patterns, price distribution patterns and overbooking strategies. The volatility of demand for all days along the booking curve are forecasted by arrival date, rate class and length of stay. It is this unprecedented level of precision that enables the e-yield system to fully optimize revenue in hotels.

The **e-yield Decision Engine** uses IDeaS unique probabilistic approach to maximize hotel revenues. Gains are achieved by selecting the optimal business mix and result from rate controls, overbooking controls, and most importantly, length-of-stay controls. These controls are based on an opportunity cost analysis and create a powerful engine that evaluates each individual room request. The analysis takes into account non-room revenues and costs (such as marginal package and distribution costs per customer) to realize maximum profit per guest. A room request is denied if the resulting revenue is less than the calculated opportunity cost.

**Decision Integration** ensures that the right reservation decisions are continually implemented. e-yield works behind the scenes with the hotel's existing reservation system, dynamically controlling available rates and length-of-stay through the familiar PMS/CRS interface. Changes in business patterns are anticipated before they occur and result in improved decision making.

What is the impact on operations?

| Affected Role | Impact |
|---|---|
| Executive Management | e-yield provides detailed reports (e.g. booking pace, history vs. demand, opportunity cost by length-of-stay, etc.) that can be used to analyze past and future business trends. |
| Yield Manager / Reservations Manager | The e-yield Full Precision Forecast and Decision Engine free the yield manager from analyzing reams of data. Instead, e-yield automates rate and length of stay restrictions as well as desired overbooking levels for the entire forecasting window. It insures that hotel yield management strategy is implemented 24 hours a day, 7 days a week. e-yield also flags exceptions (either higher or lower occupancy than expected) so that the yield manager can focus on the situation and take appropriate action. IDeaS delivers the yield manager at least a 4% increase in room revenues. |

| Affected Role | Impact |
|---|---|
| Group Sales Manager | The e-yield "group evaluation function" takes the guesswork out of signing up group business. The program determines the displacement cost of the group business so that the group sales manager can rest assured that revenue is not lost as a result of placing a group. |
| Reservationist | e-yield works with the PMS/CRS to automatically manage rates which maximize yield. Because e-yield integrates seamlessly with the PMS/CRS, the reservationist takes reservations in the normal fashion. |
| Front Desk Personnel | Full Precision Forecasting enables the property to maximize yield while closely controlling the risk of walking guests. |
| System Administrator | The e-yield system produces minimal impact to I.S. personnel because many administration tasks are handled by IDeaL/CARE staff through remote access tools. The system administrator can expect about the same amount of work as with other workstations attached to the LAN (e.g. system setup and some disk management may be required). |

# 2   IDeaL/CARE

## 2.1  What is IDeaL/CARE?

IDeaL/CARE provides the infrastructure necessary to ensure maximum yield revenue. This intricate structure of software, communications technology, issue resolution processes and highly experienced yield professionals works to insure that optimal revenue decisions are made every minute of every day – even in a rapidly changing environment.

Why go to all this trouble? Because IDeaS, like no one else, makes the 4% guarantee: we will increase revenues by at least 4% (above and beyond market forces) for all room inventory impacted by the e-yield Solution.

Delivering on this commitment requires a continuous process of monitoring, supporting, partnering and re-configuration.

1. **Monitoring** takes place via "remote computing." IDeaL/CARE staff accesses the hotel's e-yield System daily to insure that it is up and running, interacting with the PMS/CRS (property management system or central reservation system) and responding correctly to the market.

2. **Support** processes are invoked if an anomaly is discovered during monitoring or if a question or problem is submitted. Issues are logged into TROI (a database for tracking issues) and the appropriate experts are assigned. The owner of the issue follows it through to resolution and logs the results. Internal reports are generated to insure 100% resolution and that responsiveness requirements were met. You may be surprised to know that 9 out of 10 support calls actually originate from the IDeaL/CARE staff.

3. **Partnering and Re-configuration** is necessary when market conditions or business strategies change, or when major enhancements to e-yield are introduced. In these situations, hotel yield managers and IDeaS yield professionals partner to mutually understand the yield revenue situation and how to best manage it. Often times, these interactions will be initiated by IDeaS personnel as a result of "flags" generated by the system. With solution in hand, the yield professional involves the necessary IDeaS experts to re-configure and, if necessary, recalibrate the system.

IDeaL/CARE removes the element of chance from the yield management process. It insures the system is up and functioning properly, that issues are promptly resolved and that the system is properly configured given the market environment. IDeaL/CARE is an essential element of the e-yield Solution and enables us to make the 4% Guarantee.

What is included with IDeaL/CARE?

| Category | Service |
|---|---|
| Monitoring | Monitoring of e-yield and PMS Interaction |
| | Monitoring of Software Operations |
| | Decision Quality Audits |
| Support | Responding to Events/Incoming Communication |
| | Escalation to Appropriate Yield Professionals |
| | Problem/Question Resolution |
| | Patch/Update/Upgrade System |
| | Implementation of Configuration Adjustments |
| | Recalibration when Necessary |

What is the impact on operations?

| Affected Role | Impact |
|---|---|
| Executive Management | Yield management can be practiced at many levels. If you want to be the best, just as in competitive team |

| Affected Role | Impact |
|---|---|
| Yield Manager / Reservations Manager<br><br>Group Sales Manager | sports, you need talent, teamwork and practice, practice, practice. That's where IDeaS yield professionals come in. This group of hoteliers, mathematicians, scientists and engineers (many holding advanced degrees) has worked together analyzing hundreds of properties. Their goal: consistently exceed the revenue gains stated in the 4% guarantee.<br><br>When a hotel invests in IDeaL/CARE, hotel management can use this highly effective team of experts to:<br><br>• Immediately take action when yield issues arise (often before you are aware there is a problem),<br><br>• Address yield management questions,<br><br>• Partner in evaluation of yield strategy,<br><br>• Configure the e-yield system consistent with hotel strategy. |
| Information Systems Manager | IDeaL/CARE ensures the I.S. manager that e-yield System support is being performed efficiently and effectively by:<br><br>• Making support personnel available 24 hours a day, 7 days a week,<br><br>• Minimizing e-yield System down-time,<br><br>• Minimizing the need for additional staff,<br><br>• Eliminating scheduling difficulties in achieving round-the-clock support,<br><br>• Reducing the cost of training,<br><br>• Reducing the impact of employee turnover. |
| System Administrator | System administrators will appreciate the remote monitoring performed by the IDeaL/CARE staff. Tasks include:<br><br>• Daily monitoring of e-yield daily activities and software,<br><br>• Daily monitoring of system performance, |

| Affected Role | Impact |
|---|---|
| | • Daily monitoring of e-yield and PMS interaction, |
| | • Monthly monitoring to insure that archiving has been performed, |
| | • Remote installation of patches and updates as available. |
| | • If a problem is detected, the IDeaL/CARE staff invokes the support process and, when appropriate, initiates a support call to the property. |
| | This means the system administrator is free to concentrate on normal daily tasks. If a problem does arise at the hotel, the system administrator can call the IDeaL/CARE staff 24 hours a day, 7 days a week for answers or problem resolution. |
| Reservationist  Front Desk Personnel | Constant system monitoring and the IDeaL/CARE staff's commitment to 100% up time minimize the chance of the reservationist or front desk personnel being inconvenienced by system problems. |

# 3   IDeaL/RESULTS

## 3.1  What is IDeaL/RESULTS?

IDeaL/RESULTS is the *first and only tool to scientifically measure the effectiveness of a yield management system.*

The process isolates external factors such as changes in strategy or marketplace, then measures the revenue contribution solely attributable to the yield management system.

The resulting reports make it easy for hotel management to clearly evaluate the effectiveness of the product.

## 3.2  What is required?

The measurement can be performed in as little as three months following system installation. Hotel PMS/CRS (property management system or central reservation system) data must be available for the 15 months prior to installation of the system. Because only hotel PMS/CRS data is used in the analysis, IDeaL/RESULTS can evaluate any yield management system.

## 3.3 How does it work?

IDeaL/RESULTS methodology is applied to data supplied by the PMS/CRS in order to determine the change in revenue due exclusively to the yield management system. The results are presented in three separate reports: a control study, an analysis of transient business and an analysis of total business.

### 3.3.1 Control study report

The Control Study is used to validate the methodology and ensure that the benefit measurement procedure can accurately isolate any changes resulting from external factors. It does this by reporting changes in transient business for two separate periods in consecutive years.

The periods chosen represent the same time of year and are typically three months long. Both periods are *prior* to the installation of the yield management system. IDeaL/RESULTS methodology is applied to data from each period to adjust for rate and marketplace changes.

If the methods are sound, this report will show changes in transient occupancy, ADR and revPAR due to the yield management system at 0% or slightly below.

### 3.3.2 Transient business report

The Transient Business Report reviews the effect of the yield management system on transient business. As in the previous report, it uses data from the same period in two consecutive years. However in this case, one period is *prior* to system installation while the other is *after*.

The same methods, proven valid in the Control Study, are applied to the data. This time, the differences calculated are those due to the yield management system. An example of actual hotel transient revenue increases is shown below.

### 3.3.3 Total business report

This report is essentially the same as the Transient Business Report except that the overall business is reviewed. This report is important in ensuring that the yield management system does not improve transient business at the cost of some other area.

Figure 1: Actual IDeaL/RESULTS Data

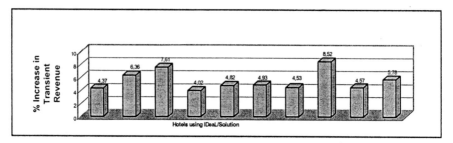

# 4 Are the results valid?

IDeaL/RESULTS methods have been reviewed by independent auditors and yield management experts. Their reviews have indicated that the methodology provides results that are both *valid and conservative*.

## 4.1 Why measure?

1. **Something may not work as expected.** Our e-yield System produces *the most accurate forecast in the industry*. It does this by properly interpreting benchmark rates, occupancy trends, out of order rooms, market segmentation, day of week patterns, length of stay patterns, historical and future block activity, booking pace patterns, price distribution patterns and overbooking strategies. It is a very thorough and complex process. We have every confidence in it, but it is possible that something may not work as we anticipate. As a company founded by scientists, we understand that. That's why we use the scientific method. We measure to insure our hypotheses are correct.

2. **You deserve value for your money.** IDeaL/RESULTS is the *first and only tool to assess yield management return on investment*. We developed it because you deserve more than a handshake to secure your interests. Not only do we measure, we back our system with the 4% guarantee: *we will increase revenues by at least 4% (above and beyond market forces) for all room inventory impacted by the e-yield Solution*.

3. **You deserve pricing choices.** IDeaL/RESULTS allows IDeaS to offer you a *unique pricing option* called Benefit Dependent Pricing (BDP). We'll do the data analysis, install the system, provide the care and perform the measurement. The price is dependent on the revenue increase produced by the system.

That's why we measure. We do it to meet our number one objective: creating measurable benefits our clients can count on.

What is the impact on operations?

| Affected Role | Impact |
|---|---|
| Executive Management<br><br>Yield Manager /<br>Reservations Manager<br><br>Group Sales Manager | Presentation of IDeaL/RESULTS takes about a day. The information allows hotel management to see how the yield system is affecting various hotel performance factors such as length of stay, occupancy, ADR and revPAR.<br><br>The information quantifies yield management system ROI. |
| System Administrator | The system administrator may be asked to provide historical PMS/CRS data. |

# 5 Hotel management

Hotel Management plays 2 critical roles in the e-yield Solution:

1. Management determines the pricing, market segment, and risk strategies which drive the solution's decision-making logic.

2. Management experience and guidance is essential in addressing unexpected market behaviour. The exception reporting system alerts management to these areas in time to take corrective actions when needed.

## 5.1 Defining the strategies that drive the decisions

Discussions with management and an analysis of the hotel are conducted before the e-yield system is built to ensure that the hotel's business policies are properly incorporated into the mathematical model; management sets the business strategies, and the e-yield Solution implements them.

An example might help demonstrate this. Suppose a hotel has a good feel for the acceptable over-booking level for a particular night, say 13 rooms. This number represents an intuitive, or perhaps spreadsheet-based, interpretation of management's underlying risk/reward strategy for overbooking. With e-yield, management quantitatively defines their overbooking risk tolerance to be consistent with the property's marketing and business goals. The system then determines how best to implement this strategy. If the system actually recommends overbooking by 25 rooms, it does so in order to accurately implement hotel management's policy while maximizing revenues.

## 5.2 Preparing for success

Executive training sessions are organized to prepare the hotel's management team for the system. The training sessions are based on the hotel's actual data. These interactive sessions, taught by IDeaS staff of specialists, also help IDeaS finalize the system calibrations. As the system is brought up, initial recommendations are tested and reviewed to build the staff's confidence in the solution. Finally, ongoing monitoring keep management in the loop at all times and exception alerts focus management's attention to the areas that need it most. Training and ongoing consulting prepare management to deal effectively with the unexpected.

Often, as a result of using the e-yield solution, management is able to spend more attention to guest services and strategic decisions such as planning, pricing, scheduling and budgeting.

Figure 2: The training steps

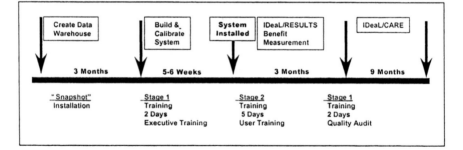

# 6 Decision integration

Decision Integration enables efficient execution of the hotel's market, risk, and pricing strategy by actually implementing the resulting reservation decisions. e-yield works through the hotel's existing reservation systems, controlling overbooking, available rates and length-of-stay through the familiar Property Management and Reservation System interfaces.

As a result, e-yield begins increasing revenues immediately after installation. The dynamic nature of the PMS (or CRS) integration also ensures that each booking and change transaction is automatically incorporated into subsequent recommendations and decisions. Instead of spending time interpreting charts and graphs to make routine reservation decisions, management is able to concentrate on more complex decisions, such as how to price and place groups, and how to set pricing. The system also produces a wide range of reports to provide the insights into demand patterns and forecasts to support mission-critical processes, such as marketing, planning, and budgeting.

When fully integrated, the hotel's revenue management practices are not subject to being compromised by staff absence, turnover or promotion. While decision integration enables effective yield management, ongoing automatic monitoring ensures its continued success.

e-yield's extensive monitoring capabilities keep hotel management in the loop at all times, directing attention where management expertise and knowledge are most needed. Decision integration and exception monitoring work hand-in-hand to provide hotel management the benefits of automation while retaining and improving decision visibility and control.

| Feature | Benefit |
| --- | --- |
| Full PMS Integration | Minimizes end-user training. |
| | Ensures decision implementation |
| | Insulates revenue management from staff turnover and absence |
| Monitoring | Directs management attention to potential problems |
| | Remote monitoring of system activity ensures smooth operations |

Printing and Binding: Strauss GmbH, Mörlenbach

Printed in the United Kingdom
by Lightning Source UK Ltd.
127458UK00003B/22-42/A